D1550505

BEHIND *the* LAUGHTER

BEHIND the LAUGHTER

A Comedian's Tale of Tragedy and Hope

ANTHONY GRIFFITH
and
BRIGITTE TRAVIS-GRIFFIN

— WITH MARK CARO —

W PUBLISHING GROUP

AN IMPRINT OF THOMAS NELSON

Published in Nashville, Tennessee, by W Publishing Group, an imprint of Thomas Nelson.

Thomas Nelson titles may be purchased in bulk for educational, business, fund-raising, or sales promotional use. For information, please e-mail SpecialMarkets@ThomasNelson.com.

Unless otherwise noted, Scripture quotations are taken from the King James Version. Public domain.

Scripture quotations marked NIV are from the Holy Bible, New International Version®, NIV®. © 1973, 1978, 1984, 2011 by Biblica, Inc.® Used by permission of Zondervan. All rights reserved worldwide.

Any Internet addresses, phone numbers, or company or product information printed in this book are offered as a resource and are not intended in any way to be or to imply an endorsement by Thomas Nelson, nor does Thomas Nelson vouch for the existence, content, or services of these sites, phone numbers, companies, or products beyond the life of this book.

ISBN 978-0-7852-1981-1 (eBook)

Library of Congress Cataloging-in-Publication Data

Names: Griffith, Anthony, author. | Travis-Griffin, Brigitte, author. | Caro, Mark, author.
Title: Behind the laughter : a comedian's tale of tragedy and hope / Anthony Griffith and Brigitte Travis-Griffin; with Mark Caro.
Description: Nashville, Tennessee: W Publishing, an imprint of Thomas Nelson, [2019] | Identifiers: LCCN 2018048771 (print) | LCCN 2018056198 (eBook) | ISBN 9780785219507 (hardcover) | ISBN 9780785219811 (eBook)
Subjects: LCSH: Griffith, Anthony. | Comedians—United States—Biography. | African American comedians—Biography. | Daughters—United States—Death. | Fathers and daughters—United States.
Classification: LCC PN2287.G698 (ebook) | LCC PN2287.G698 A3 2019 (print) | DDC 792.7/6028092 [B] —dc23
LC record available at https://lccn.loc.gov/2018048771

Printed in the United States of America

19 20 21 22 23 24 LSC 8 7 6 5 4 3 2 1

Contents

PROLOGUE

Standing on the Star

"Would you welcome, please . . ."

Anthony

On the most exciting day of my career in the worst year of my life, I stood atop a star on a stage, with three big cameras thrust in my face and an audience of six hundred people stacked behind them. To my left blared Doc Severinsen and his big band. To my right, so much closer than I could have imagined, sat Johnny Carson.

When I was growing up on Chicago's South Side, these were not sights and sounds that I ever thought I'd experience. *The Tonight Show Starring Johnny Carson* came from an exotic-sounding place called Burbank, California, and showed up on the big black-and-white console TV that I watched as a kid. This was where I saw the biggest stars, from Muhammad Ali to John Wayne, chatting with the man who put America to bed each night. Johnny told jokes, played with animals, and portrayed goofy characters, such as the psychic Carnac the Magnificent. I noticed that Johnny got some of his biggest laughs when his material bombed.

I didn't see any escape artists or magicians on the show, and that's what I wanted to be when I was young. That Johnny started out as a magician was something I learned later. When I began performing stand-up comedy in my college years in the early '80s, *The Tonight Show* became more relevant to me.

For an aspiring comic, that was *the* show. Johnny Carson was the king of late-night television no matter who challenged him, and he launched generations of careers via the six-minute sets that he introduced.

Still, for this tall black kid who started out in the projects, *The Tonight Show* was something that happened on TV, not in real life. People from where I grew up never think they're going to be on television. That world is and was so foreign and out of reach. Burbank might as well have been on the moon.

In a blue-collar family like mine, the goal was to get a good government job. The post office—that was it. That was security. That was "Ooh, I've made it." People in my family and community did that for decades. To venture off that grid to work in stand-up—well, my mom didn't understand that, though she was as supportive as she could be.

"This is good, Tony," she said, "and when you get it out of your system, you can get a government job." Then she prayed for me.

I had no idea how to pursue getting on *The Tonight Show*. There was no one to help steer my path toward Hollywood. All I knew was how to make people laugh, so that's what I tried to do everywhere I could.

And, somehow, I wound up standing on this star.

My wife, Brigitte, couldn't join me at the studio, though she had worked hard to get me to this point as well. She had to be home with our two-year-old daughter, Brittany. I thought everything would be fine. We had done all right so far. I was the optimist.

Plus, I had other things to be nervous about. I didn't want to embarrass myself in front of my family. I didn't want to embarrass myself in front of my community. And I didn't want to embarrass myself in front of the eighteen million people who would be watching me through those camera lenses.

One of the most familiar, trusted voices in America had said these words:

Here's a young man making his very first appearance on *The Tonight Show*.
He's a stand-up comedian from Chicago . . .

Now I was on my spot.
The red light atop the camera was on.
I was living every comic's dream.
With a nightmare attached.

Losing the Straitjacket

My grandmother's eyesight has gotten bad, so she
always thinks somebody's trying to break in the house.
"I see a shadow."
"Put the gun down."
"But I see a shadow, baby."'
"I know you do. You got cataracts."

Anthony

While I was growing up, my house was a no-swear zone. I don't remember my mom or stepfather ever swearing. Mom was a devout Christian, a preacher's daughter, so she raised us the way she grew up: no cussing allowed. When I was a senior in high school, I would say, "Man, kiss my ankle," because I couldn't say, "Kiss my butt." If I used that word at all, I had to spell it out, "B-U-T-T." Once my brother and I were having an argument, and I *did* say, "Man, I'll kick your butt," and my mom gave me the death look, and I knew I'd never do that again.

So I'd be in school, trying to act tough, saying, "Kiss my ankle," "Kiss my derriere," "Kiss my buttocks," and people would go, "What? You cray." I wasn't scaring anyone.

By the time I got into the comedy clubs, everyone was swearing. I would try to swear, but I couldn't do it. It was like someone trying to speak English for the first time. I didn't mean to become known as the Comedian Who Doesn't Swear. It was just part of my upbringing.

Born in 1962, I grew up on Chicago's South Side after starting out in the West Side projects. My little brother, Danny, and I left there with my mom to flee my biological father because of his drinking issues and his treatment of her. I was five, and Danny was three.

Our West Side apartment had green painted walls and a lot of brick, and it was pretty nice. The projects back then were relatively new and clean. They were designed for young families just starting out, and families were pretty big back then, so the apartments had four or five bedrooms. The idea was that as the residents got better jobs and made more money, they would move out of the projects, and new families would move in, though it didn't really work out that way.

I had relatives living on different floors within the complex and also on nearby blocks, including in the townhomes down the street. With family members scattered throughout the neighborhood, I felt safe as a kid even when my parents were at work. It was a community. People didn't worry about kids being snatched, and we trusted our neighbors, so I ran alone to preschool and kindergarten, both in the same nearby building, and it was no big deal.

Our television set must have weighed five hundred pounds. I watched a lot of TV, starting the day with the cartoon/variety show *Ray Rayner and His Friends* on WGN Channel 9. Something that confused me about TV was that the same person might appear on two different channels at the same time. How did that happen? When I saw someone on both Channel 2 and Channel 5, I turned the knob between them to try to catch him.

We had a fake Christmas tree every winter and nothing fancy for dinner most days. Mom served up sugar bread, syrup bread, hot-sauce bread, and ketchup bread, and sometimes we had fried bologna or fried salami. These were staples of low-income life, but we weren't uncomfortable. I didn't consider that I was poor until we started getting government lunches at school and I realized that not every family needed them. Government lunches were not good. We got bologna sandwiches containing slabs of butter that were thicker than the meat; kids threw these disgusting sandwiches away. But we always had one piece of fruit, like an apple or an orange, plus a Fig Newton. Then there were government cheese and government milk, so on top of being poor, we were constipated.

Something I hated as a kid was being sent to the grocery store with food stamps because I had to tell the cashier, "I have food stamps." That signified that our family was on government assistance, and the cashiers were loud about it. If I forgot to mention the stamps before the cashiers rang up everything, they shouted, "How come you didn't tell me you were on food stamps?" That made me feel small.

Each morning the Black Panthers served a full, hot breakfast at school as part of their community outreach. The Panthers were a big presence in the late '60s. Chicago was very divided, and in the black neighborhoods, you had the gangs, and you had the revolutionaries. It was the era of Black Power, and a lot of people were talking about freedom, wanting their voices heard, challenging the status quo. Everybody had big Afros, and even the hair picks had a revolutionary theme; they were red, green, and black, the colors of the Pan-African/Black Liberation flag. The untold story of the Panthers is that they were great cooks.

Both of my parents were born in Chicago, but their families came up from the South during the Great Migration in the first half of the twentieth century, so I have roots in Mississippi, New Orleans, and Oklahoma. My mom, Sharon Griffin, grew up on the West Side as one of nine kids. She was cross-eyed and beautiful, comparable to Lena Horne or Halle Berry. She was regal, likable, approachable, and smart as a whip, the valedictorian of her class at Crane High School. She carried herself elegantly, but if you pushed her, she'd remind you that she was from the projects. She knew how to defend herself. If she ever felt backed into a corner, she would fight for her life, and you'd probably have to kill her to get her to stop.

During one of the times when my biological father threw my mom over his shoulder to carry her into the bedroom, where we couldn't see what he'd do to her, she pitched forward and grabbed him where it counts and wouldn't let go. She squeezed with all her might.

"Let go!" he yelled, but she knew if she did, it would be over.

"I was not gonna let go," she recounted to my brother and me years later, all of us laughing to the point of tears.

He was threatening her with "You better let me go!" and "When I get you . . .," but he was in pain and howling and bucking like a bronco. Soon he was on his knees, whimpering, "I'm telling you . . ." before he passed out. She almost got arrested because he was the property of the military—he was in the army—and he was damaged goods for a week or two.

"Why would he beat me?" she said. "I was the person in his corner."

The final straw came when my father pulled a knife on my mom. We were in the living room, and my mom had had enough, so she broke two glasses and held them out in front of her, shouting, "If this is going to happen, let's get this over with!"

My brother was crying on the couch, and I was crying too. I was old enough to know that something bad was going on, though I didn't know exactly what. It was a standoff that ended with my father turning and going into the bedroom.

When he went to sleep off his alcohol-fueled rage, my mom grabbed me and my brother and got out of there. She took no money, no food, and no clothing. We went to the South Side to be with Big Momma and her two dogs and her .38 Special.

Big Momma was my mom's mom, and Danny and I lay on the floor of her house as gunfire rang out—because it was midnight on New Year's Eve, and Big Momma was firing her gun out the window to celebrate. She was like that.

Years later I talked about this onstage:

I was at my grandmother's house one year for New Year's Eve.
I counted twenty bullet holes in her window—ten from my
grandmother shooting back.

After she'd hear me tell these jokes, she'd complain, "Why are you always lying?"

"I'm not lying," I'd reply. "You *do* have a gun around the house. You *do* chew tobacco."

In fact, she used to sit at her spot in the living room and spit into a can she kept on the table beside her. Big Momma wasn't *that* big, though when you're a little kid, everyone seems big. She wasn't as tall as my mom, who was about five feet nine, but she wasn't as slender either.

My grandmother is what they call a big-boned woman. I don't mind
a big-boned woman, but spandex isn't for everybody.

I think of her as always having gray hair, though it must have been darker at some point. Our favorite meal of hers was chitlins, corn bread, and greens, which we ate with our hands.

Big Momma was always nice to me, and I spent much time sitting on her lap as her big picture of Jesus looked at us. It was your typical warm, loving Jesus portrait, like you'd see in stores, but one element made me uneasy. It hung in the kitchen, which was open to the living room, so no matter where I was in the house, I could feel Jesus' eyes following me.

Big Momma's house was off Eighty-Seventh Street, not far from the Dan Ryan Expressway, which cuts through the South Side of Chicago. There were two bedrooms, both on one floor (a separate, second-floor apartment could be reached from the back), so Big Momma and Big Daddy had one bedroom, Mom stayed in the other one, and Danny and I slept on a rollaway bed in the living room. Big Daddy was not my mom's dad or Big Momma's first husband, and we rarely saw him. He was a security guard who worked weird hours, mostly at night, and kept vicious guard dogs in the backyard, so we were never allowed to go back there.

My mom found work a few miles to the north in Hyde Park, a relatively integrated neighborhood that's home to the University of Chicago. She rented a separate apartment there to spare herself the commute during the week, but landlords in the '60s didn't want to rent to single moms, especially black ones, so when we went to visit her, we had to pretend that we were her nephews.

My mom eventually brought Danny and me to live with her in a Hyde Park apartment on Fifty-Third Street above a dry cleaner. There was only one bedroom, so she let us have it, and she slept in the living room. She was always sacrificing. Then we moved to another apartment in Hyde Park, and again Mom gave us the bedroom, and she lived in the front of the apartment. By the time we moved to another apartment, she was remarried, and she and my stepdad took the bedroom, and we slept up front. This was my new father: a hardworking, blue-collar guy named Fred Johnson, asserting his authority and saying, "I ain't sleepin' in front."

I went to grade school in Hyde Park and then high school at the Kenwood Academy. In grade school we had busing without a bus; I had to walk about a mile and a half to school. In high school we had a track team without a track.

We had to run in the hallways. The schools in the suburbs where we competed had three gyms, a big Olympic track, and a pool.

Hyde Park was a positive for our family. Mom liked it as a community and felt this was where she could raise her kids. We could enjoy a quality of life there superior to what we'd experienced on the poverty-stricken West and Far South sides. Wealthy people lived in Hyde Park, among the middle and lower classes. The University of Chicago added to the community's cultural richness, as did the Museum of Science and Industry and other institutions. And at a time of pronounced segregation in Chicago, Hyde Park offered racial and ethnic diversity, showing the possibilities of a new America melting and mingling as one.

Hyde Park was the first place where I interacted with white people. Before then I'd seen white people only on TV. Whites didn't go into black neighborhoods in Chicago, and vice versa. It was confusing for me. Who were these people?

My new white friends had names such as John and Arthur. My friends with whom I'd grown up were called Goo Goo, Cadillac, and Pony. I knew maybe only a fourth of my black friends' actual birth names. Someone called Skillet might really be Bartholomew. These were the names you heard in the inner city. If you were introduced to Ice Tray, Junebug, or Pookie, you just thought, *Okay, that's his name.*

My birth name was Anthony Griffin, no middle name. The professional switch to Griffith came years later. I was originally going to be named John H. Griffin, after my biological father, but even then my mom thought no, no, no. So I wasn't named after anyone.

My family called me Tony unless I was in trouble, and then I was Anthony. My teachers called me Anthony. My friends and just about everybody in the neighborhood called me Griff. On the playground, on the basketball courts, at the Y, they'd say, "Griff, what's up?"

Because my hair was wavy, some people would ask my mom, "What's your daughter's name?" I would get so mad and say, "I'm not a girl." But I had a lot of hair, and I was pretty.

Then came my Afro. I was proud of my 'fro, and the people who cut and styled it were too. When I was in grade school, they'd enter me in hair shows. They would rent out a hall or community center, and hundreds of people would attend as the barbers and stylists showed off their work and sold hair-care products. (This sort of thing still goes on today, and it's even more elaborate.) The barber would ask my mother if he could put me in one of these shows, and then he'd do my hair. I was like his walking business card.

A couple of my white friends had Afros too. Everyone had a lot of hair in the late '60s and early '70s.

I loved Hyde Park because it introduced me to different cultures. I grew up with every ethnic and religious group: blacks, whites, Asians, Mexicans, Muslims, Jewish people, and more. Some of my Jewish friends collected and traded stamps, so I did too. I also liked putting together models of the monsters that we saw on *Creature Features*, like Dracula, the Wolf Man, and the Mummy. I never thought I was a nerd until I was around my fellow brothers, and they'd react to my hobbies by saying, "Griff, come on, man."

At a sleepover once my friends made fun of me because I brought my homework. Didn't everybody?

"No, Griff. We're sleeping over. We're not doing our homework this weekend."

I was not a street kid even though I grew up in the inner city. I was naive to the tenth power.

My mom didn't want my brother or me anywhere near the gangs or other kinds of trouble, so she made the YMCA our refuge. "When you get out of school, you go directly to the Y," she said. There were no ifs, ands, or buts. She signed us up for every available class there: floor hockey, basketball, gymnastics, martial arts, swimming. The counselors knew us by name, and we sort of grew up there. When my mom was done with her workday, she picked us up.

She also walked us to the library in Hyde Park, where they showed old black-and-white movies on the weekend. She enrolled us in Cub Scouts and Boy Scouts as well. I hated Boy Scouts because gang members were in it, and the troop leader was afraid of them. They took over. My troop never learned to fish. We never did anything. I have the cooking badge and a bunch of others, but we got them because the scoutmaster was scared of the gang members, not because we actually earned them.

Yet as tough as the gang members were on the street, they got scared when we went into the woods. They were afraid to go to the outhouse.

"Griff, go with me, man."

"Come on. You're just going to the bathroom."

They knew the inner city but not camp life.

The gangs eventually approached me about joining, but the general rule was you either were a gang member or an athlete, and I looked the part of an athlete. I was lean and tall and knew how to play basketball, so they left me alone. I actually wanted to be a hockey player, but I was a terrible skater. The coach said, "I love your enthusiasm, but you've got to be able to skate backwards." I couldn't. So I played basketball—in the rain, in the cold, in the winter. You would play, play, play until your mom called you in.

I never swam before I was in Hyde Park. In the projects your pool was the fire hydrant. When I got to Hyde Park, it was white people, and it was swimming. I remember the first time I tried it. All the kids were jumping into the pool. I saw the white kids swimming, so I thought people were just born knowing how to do that. But when I jumped into the water, I went straight down.

I was screaming for my mom. I thought I was going to die.

"Stand up!" the lifeguard yelled.

I did. Turned out I was in the shallow end.

Then there was church. When my brother and I were little, church started in the home at 6:00 or 6:30 on Sunday mornings with my mom singing gospel songs to clear the air of any evil spirits that might have lingered from Saturday night. She sang only church songs at home, and she prepared all of the day's food on Saturday because Sunday was set aside as the day of the Lord. We dressed up and went to church services that began at 7:00 a.m.

Once we were living in Hyde Park, there was a white family, the Brubakers, who picked up the neighborhood kids and drove us to their Baptist church on the South Side. Mr. Brubaker was the pastor, and Mrs. Brubaker was our grade school music teacher, and they had two biological children plus an adopted Mexican girl and a Native American girl. They were really cool. They'd fit Danny and me and six other kids into a VW van and take us from Hyde Park to the church a few miles south. We attended Sunday school, and afterward they treated us to White Castle as a reward, though the only time I'd had a slider was when I had the twenty-four-hour flu, so I didn't go for the burgers.

Sunday school was fun because we were with our friends. We got baptized at that church.

I consider myself likable, approachable, warm, and friendly, yet my mom passed along some of her tough qualities to me. If I ever feel threatened, I get real quiet, I get real still, and my instincts kick in.

I've had only three fights in my life, and the last one was in high school. When I was growing up, people equated being nice with being weak, and they set out to test you. (This turned out to be true in Hollywood too.) In school we had something called the "game of chest": you allow the person to hit you, and then you hit the person, and it goes on like that until someone gives up. So the guy hits you in your chest as hard as he can, and if he knocks you down or you cry or you say, "Please, please," he knows he can control you. You're a punk to him.

I must've been sixteen or seventeen when this one guy, he was provoking me, itching for a fight, acting like, *Yeah, I'm gonna take Anthony and show that he's a punk.*

There was a big crowd chanting, "Fight! Fight! Fight!"

My opponent hit me, and then I hit him back, and he hit me, and I hit him back. It went on and on like this for so long that people started leaving. They were like, *Wait—they're going to keep doing this?* I think we were at it for more than an hour. Kids would go and come back, saying, "You're still here?"

I was hurting, but I knew that if I stopped, he'd think I was a punk. He would've said, "Give me your lunch money," and all that. So I kept hitting, he kept hitting, and I kept hitting, until he finally said, "All right." We shook hands. It was like "You passed the test." I was trying to put him down, but I've never been the strongest guy or the biggest guy, though I've always been tall. My strength is my inner strength.

I think I was drawn to comedy for a simple reason: I loved to laugh, and I loved to make people laugh. I got that from my mom too.

I was never the class clown. And I would never do the "yo mama" jokes. I always had a sensitive spirit, so I couldn't be talking about your mom. When someone tried to insult me with one of those jokes, I would just die because I couldn't retaliate.

But my friends thought I was silly. I *was* silly. I was always doing impressions of John Wayne and Elvis Presley.

In my early teens I didn't want to be a comedian. I wanted to be a magician. I had this trick where you light a fire in a dish, and you cover the dish, and then you open the dish, and—voilà!—there's a dove. The problem was, I didn't know where to find a dove in the city, so instead I borrowed my friend's parakeet.

While I was trying to do this trick, the parakeet wouldn't stay down in the container, and he kept biting me. This bird was a jerk, and he wouldn't stop talking.

"Shut up," I finally said.

"*You* shut up," the parakeet shot back.

Now, when I speak to kids, I give them this advice: "When you're a magician, you have to follow the instructions. If the instructions say, 'Use a dove,' use a dove."

I tried performing magic at my eighth-grade talent show, but none of my tricks were working. "I'm going to get this trick to work, or we're going to be here all night," I said, frustrated.

The kids laughed at that. I didn't think it was funny because I was just trying not to mess up. But I did notice that I was better at getting laughs than at performing magic.

For a while I envisioned myself as a modern-day Houdini. When Johnny Carson was a teenage magician, he called himself "the Great Carsoni." I called myself "the Great Griffini." One year I asked my mom for a straitjacket for Christmas. Sure enough, what did I find under the Christmas tree? My very own straitjacket. You could buy straitjackets in magic stores, and they were different from the actual ones—easier to get out of, for one. But my mom didn't know that, so she went to a mental hospital and convinced them to sell her one.

When I told people I'd gotten a straitjacket for Christmas, they thought I was crazy, but I appreciated how far my mom would go to make her kid happy.

Pretty soon I knew how to get out of not only the straitjacket but handcuffs and chains too.

After I conquered my water fears, I went with some friends to the Y pool one afternoon after school. The plan was to have them chain me up, push me into the deep end, and watch as I miraculously escaped.

"Can I do this?" I asked the lifeguard.

"No, stupid. Get out of here," he said.

Plan B was to do it anyway.

"Chain me up, I'll jump in, and if you see bubbles, come get me," I told my friends.

We went to the edge of the pool, my friends distracted the lifeguard, and into the water I went. I managed to wriggle out of the chains. Yeah, I was a weird kid, but I had an inner circle of friends who liked me and my goofiness, and that's what counted.

A lot of people at school didn't believe that I was a magician and escape artist, so I'd take my straitjacket to school to demonstrate. One day I left it at the bus stop, and by the time I got back there, it was gone. Who steals a straitjacket? People in Chicago.

When I asked my stepdad whether I could have another straitjacket, he looked at me as if I'd asked for a rocket to the moon. He didn't even bother replying.

That was the end of my magic career. From then on I had to entertain people with my words instead of with props.

2

Finding Laughter and Love

I was a butler in plays that didn't have butlers. I was a
butler in *West Side Story.*

Brigitte

Who is sleeping at seven thirty in the morning at work? Who does that?

Somebody who's been out partying, that's who.

This guy was dozing in the cafeteria of the luxury hotel where we both worked. I was a supervisor at the Park Hyatt—one of Chicago's prime addresses along the Magnificent Mile—overlooking the historic Water Tower and, beyond that, Lake Michigan. I'd worked hard to get to where I was. This place had standards, and so did I.

I'll give him this: he was handsome. Absolutely. He was tall, slim, and I loved the way he carried himself. He had kind of a cool, quiet confidence about him.

There was one other thing I liked about him: his shoes. I can tell a lot about someone from his shoes. If you look like you've been kicking flour, I don't want to have anything to do with you because that's a detail you should have taken care of. Before you come out of your home, look at your shoes, and if it looks like you've been kicking flour, get right back in there and dust them puppies off. This guy's shoes were never like that. He wore a lovely pair of leather dress shoes that looked like they were made of butter.

Just aesthetically speaking, I was attracted to him. Other than that, though, I did not like this man. His behavior rubbed me the wrong way.

I enjoyed having breakfast at the hotel's cafeteria downstairs. Employees were treated so nicely there, and the food was awesome. One of the cooks was my friend and took great care of me, but when I would see this guy in the back, nodding off, I'd lose my glow. It was unprofessional to be dozing in a semipublic environment at 7:30 a.m. He'd obviously been out drinking, dancing—whatever. He was probably coming to work from some woman's house.

He was a valet parker and also worked as a doorman. He would open the door for me as I came and went. When he saw me walking toward him at the hotel, he would say hello.

Sorry, not interested.

"Hello," I'd mutter as I passed him by.

Anthony

Even though I was tired from getting up at 3:30 a.m. to take my long walk to the bus stop every day, I had to be alert. I never knew when I'd have to outrun the stray dogs. It was still dark out, and almost always cold, as I fast-walked to a soundtrack of barking. Some of these yapping dogs were gated in yards, but more ran loose, and I knew that at any moment I might have to sprint for the bus while they closed in on me.

My daily commute was a pain but not atypical for someone living on the South Side. On the North Side, which generally has more money and diversity (and white people) than the South or West sides, the "L" train and bus lines were never far away. The city had made public transportation less of a priority for the neighborhoods south and west of the Loop, especially those that were poor and black. We also were the last ones to see snowplows and salt trucks in the winter, at least until Harold Washington became Chicago's first black mayor in 1983.

After graduating from Kenwood Academy, I enrolled at Northeastern Illinois University on Chicago's far Northwest Side. I was good at numbers— thanks to my mom teaching me lots of math shortcuts when I was a kid—so I had planned to become an accountant and majored in accounting. After seeing a notice posted on the school's bulletin board, I got an accounting job nearby. That office was the destination of my morning public transportation adventures.

I was still living at home with my parents. We had moved farther south to near Eighty-Ninth Street, so I had to take a bus to the Ninety-Fifth Street station, which was the end of the line, next to the Dan Ryan Expressway, before I headed north. At the back of the bus, some guys ran a three-card monte game, and I had to stay awake, or keep at least one eye open, because I didn't want to get robbed.

Even though it was still early when I got to the "L" station, it felt like rush hour, bustling with an entire service industry's worth of riders going downtown or to the North Side for any number of jobs as nurses, salesclerks, mechanics, cleaning women, lawn-care workers. My stepfather—who worked as a custodian, taxi driver, and handyman, basically doing anything to put food on the table—was up and gone by the time I got out of bed.

All the folks converging on the station were the clientele of the hustlers selling whatever might be needed that day. Before there was Walmart, there was the "L" stop, where you could buy anything and everything for a discount. If it was going to rain, they had umbrellas. If it was cold, they had mittens. You could get long johns and hats, as well as toiletries and baby shoes. Who didn't go shopping at a train station for baby shoes?

After riding the "L" north, I transferred trains downtown. I associate that part of the trip with the urine stink that permeated the underground walkway. By the time I rode to the north end of what then was called the Ravenswood Line (and now is known as the Brown Line), the vibe had changed. The nasty smells gave way to the aroma from street cleaners, and people were walking to work with a sense of purpose. It felt like a brand-new day.

I still had to take another bus to reach the accounting office. Starbucks wasn't around back then, and I don't drink coffee anyway, so I was slowly waking up, getting my wits about me. By the time I arrived at 7:00 a.m., I'd been awake for three and a half hours.

Aside from the commute, my day included my job and my college classes, and I was also on the school's basketball team. My life was packed. Yet, it turned out, I had time for something else. When I saw a play at Northeastern, my desire to become an entertainer was rekindled. It was a comedy. The actors weren't telling jokes, but I was hearing laughs. That made me feel good.

I started taking classes in the theater department, and after my sophomore year, I switched my major from accounting to communication, with a minor in theater. I didn't tell my parents. My stepfather didn't understand why I wanted to go to college in the first place.

"Start life," he'd said.

But I'm still communicating, so there.

I had another hard choice to make. I had too many commitments and was still playing basketball although I'd enjoyed it more in high school than in college. I had to get real: No one was going to name gym shoes after me. I wasn't headed to the pros. It was time to wrap it up.

I was distraught about telling the coach. I hate breaking bad news to people. What would I say?

Finally, I approached him. "Coach, I don't think I can do this anymore."

"Okay," he said.

That was it. I'd thought he'd say, "Oh, Anthony, we really want to keep you," but I guess I wasn't that great a player.

My friends were jocks, and I didn't really know anybody in theater. I went from talking sports with my buddies to building sets and acting. I felt at home in both worlds, but after I committed to the theater program, I blossomed. Northeastern is a small school, and the theater department was small, too, unlike the massive one at nearby Northwestern University. The community at Northeastern was tight, and everyone was nice.

As the only black theater student for much of my time at Northeastern, I did encounter a few obstacles. I tried out for shows, but few directors employed nontraditional casting at the time, and most of the lead roles were assumed to be white. Now many shows are multicultural, such as *Hamilton*, and even revivals of the classics often get cast with an eye on diversity, but back when we were doing *Oklahoma!* on campus, no one thought about having a black cowboy.

So no matter how strong my audition, I was never the lead. I was a dancer and singer in *Oklahoma!* and the same pattern followed for shows such as *South Pacific* and *Annie Get Your Gun*, in which I played a waiter on a train. When we did *Othello*, I thought, *Here's my chance.* But the directors brought in another, older black actor from outside the school to play the lead. (I'm actually glad I didn't star in *Othello* then because I had no understanding of

Shakespeare. By the time I did play Othello years later in a Los Angeles in-the-park production, I had more knowledge and experience under my belt.)

When friends from the inner city would come to see me in a play, I'd be wearing tights and makeup, and they'd say, "Man, Griff, you're strange." But I was having fun. I really enjoyed college. I was expanding my horizons, meeting different kinds of people. My fellow theater students and I participated in competitions in Madison, Wisconsin, and other places unfamiliar to me. This was a world I didn't know, but I was happy for the new experiences. I think I was one of two males in my dance class. I was eighteen, nineteen, twenty, so why not?

Having switched my major, there was no point in keeping the accounting job, so while still in college, I started working at the Park Hyatt. If anything, my schedule got even more insane. I began as a carhop on the graveyard shift, which ended at 7:00 or 7:30 a.m., at which point I'd hop the "L" toward school.

I was working at the hotel when a supervisor in another department caught my eye. She was tall, dark, with long hair and huge '80s glasses. I mean *huge*. They were goofy, but she was not. She was a force. From the moment she arrived at the hotel, she was in forward motion. I was taking shifts as a doorman, and she would walk right by me on the way to her office. She didn't linger, didn't shoot the breeze. She was a woman on a mission.

She was six feet tall, and I wouldn't say I was intimidated because I'm six feet four, but I thought, *Man, that's a* woman! She looked like Jayne Kennedy or Vanessa Williams—stunning, beautiful. In college you see a lot of young ladies, but this was something else. This woman had it together. Who was I? A lowly car hiker/bellman. Two different worlds.

Even with all of my performing experience, I remained painfully shy around women. For years I was so bashful that girls thought I was conceited. I couldn't talk to them even though I would have loved to. If a girl made fun of me, I said, "Awww," and withdrew. If I went across the gym to ask a girl to dance and she said no, I was done for the whole night. It was like I'd gotten a divorce even if I didn't know the girl. "No" to me sounded like this: "*NOOOOOOOOO!*" It was as if she had not only turned me down but also distributed flyers about me to every other girl in school.

In my teenage and young adult years, I was attracted to women who had little use for someone like me. I wanted the girl who wanted the bad boy, and

I was never the bad boy. I was always told, "Naw, you too nice." My through line in life was "You too nice." I wanted women to think I was one of those cool guys, but I still had to spell out "B-U-T-T." The bad-boy thing wasn't happening.

Little did I know that this hotel supervisor, named Brigitte, was turned off by me because she thought I was some sort of playboy. That's funnier than any of the jokes I was telling at the time.

The Park Hyatt is where I launched my comedy career. The hotel hosted an employee talent show, and I made that show the test: I'd perform a stand-up routine, and if it went well—if people laughed—then I'd take my chances in the comedy clubs around Chicago.

In my mind there wasn't a big distinction between performing in a play and doing stand-up. In both cases I was onstage, entertaining people. But with stand-up, a director didn't get to decide which role I'd play, and I didn't have to express myself through other people's words. I could come up with my own stories, my own jokes, drawn from my own life. I didn't have to write anything down. I kept it all in my head.

During that time, my jokes were pretty corny. I wasn't advanced as a storyteller. I did a lot of impressions—of people working at the hotel as well as of celebrities. I imitated Mr. T (working as a hotel housekeeper) and Michael Jackson. I also pretended to meet with a hotel supervisor who wanted to move me up to management, but I argued that I'd rather be a bellhop because that's where the real money was. Some of those guys would make $100 to $150 in tips, so that wasn't really a joke.

At the end of the talent show, I was declared the winner and received a bottle of champagne, which I would never drink because I didn't. Some of my female coworkers took notice of my triumph. At a party afterward, one young lady who worked in the kitchen was standing close to me on the stairwell, saying, "You were real funny. Hee-hee." She was gorgeous and showing a lot of cleavage—just the sort of woman who was never interested in me. Well, hello! I was enjoying the attention.

At that moment Brigitte, who wasn't even at the talent show, walked past me and gave me the evil eye. What was *her* problem?

Of course, nothing happened with the woman from the kitchen that night or afterward. The next day I went up to her, thinking we had a connection. She was like, "Excuse me?"

"I'm the guy last night who was doing comedy."

"And?"

That was that. She was giving me the "Naw, you too nice" look.

I stunk at interpreting the signs between men and women. If you were female and smiled at me, I thought, *Yeah, she likes me.* Then my brother would say, "Dude, that's the waitress. She smiles so she can get a tip." Oh.

Winning the talent show, nonetheless, gave me the courage to go out to the local clubs and bars. Would other people think I was funny? This was a great time to find out.

In the early to mid-1980s, comedy was the big thing. It was all over TV, including cable channels that were beginning to grow in popularity, and every bar, restaurant, or nightclub had found a way to showcase it. One club in Rosemont, near O'Hare International Airport, was called the Comedy Cottage, and it was packed every night. People would sit in the aisles. That's where I started.

Comedians performed for free, and if they did well, they'd get $2.00 a show. If they did *really* well, they moved up to $5.00 a show, then $7.50, and finally, if they made it up to becoming an emcee, $10.00. When I did that, I was like, *Wow, $10.00! You can't stop me! Hold me back!*

I also worked at the Comedy Womb in west suburban Elmhurst, which paid $5.00 a show, and other places that comics told me about, such as Barrel of Laughs in south suburban Oak Lawn. I was at ground level and didn't mind. I would perform anywhere and everywhere. The clubs were conducive to comedy because people drank and got loud, so they were ready to laugh. But I also had to work to keep their attention. I would play the openings of restaurants, nightclubs, bars, and other lowly gigs. It was a great learning experience as I worked all over Chicago as well as Wisconsin and Indiana.

I was also still in college, taking classes and acting there and in productions at little black box theaters around town. I enjoyed both stand-up and acting even if I wasn't making money doing either. My aim was to learn my craft and to meet people. Sometimes I'd do a gig before my graveyard shift at the Park Hyatt and after work go straight to my morning classes. I was whupped. The teacher for my first class of the day was sympathetic and would let me nod off. He was one of the theater department professors, so he knew what I was going through.

Brigitte, however, did not.

She wasn't my supervisor; as I said earlier, we were in different departments. Still, we would see each other every day. She would come into the cafeteria at breakfast time, and I'd be dozing off, convincing her I'd been out all night. Seeing me chatting up that woman after the talent show only confirmed her suspicions that I was trying to live the wild life: *He's trying to get her number. He's a dog.*

Brigitte

I didn't go to the hotel talent show because I still thought Anthony was a player. To tell the truth, I had sworn off black guys and was dating guys from other ethnic backgrounds. I had a stereotyped impression of black men, and he was fitting the mold, even though my friend Diane had told me, "You know, he's a really nice guy. If he looks your way, just acknowledge him."

No, thank you.

I wasn't interested in seeing any of my other coworkers perform in the show either, so I chose to work that night instead but arranged to get together after my shift and the show with some friends who'd been there. We all were going up the stairs when I saw this cute girl talking to Anthony. He was leaning in with this big grin on his face. If he had died right there and fallen into her ample bosom, he would have achieved bliss. She was giggling, and it sounded like this: "*Kee kee kee kee!*"

"Ugh. Please," I said to my friends, "let's go."

"No, no, let's ask Tony if he wants to come with us," they said.

"Come on," I said. "See there? I told you he was a player. Why are you guys trying to hook me up with another black man?"

"He's a nice guy."

"Well, that's nice that he's nice."

"You should talk to him."

"I'm not talking to him."

"But he's very respectful. He's a sweet guy."

Too bad. I had no interest in him.

Eventually my girlfriends wore me down, and I decided to give him a chance. In the '80s companies would throw these big office parties, and we had one at a disco club on Rush Street. I invited Tony because it felt relatively safe. That's when I started getting to know him. We had a nice talk that night, and I soon invited him over for dinner at my apartment in Rogers Park, the city's northernmost neighborhood, along the lake.

What do you know? He was so nice. He loved his mom. He was a Christian. He had awesome core values.

He was almost the opposite of me in terms of energy. He was very laid-back and didn't talk much—yet on those first few dates, we stayed out just talking and talking. Now I can't get him to shut up. And even though he was a bashful guy, he liked being around people. I'm just the opposite. I'm an introvert, but I can turn it on for the masses, and then when I get home, I'm exhausted. He had a calming effect on me. I also have a potty mouth, and he doesn't. To get him to swear—he won't do it unless it's in a script and he has no choice.

So we complemented each other, and I really appreciated that. When you're in your twenties, you do things on principle, and you'll die before you acquiesce to anyone else's opinion. That's how I was, and he was the opposite. I liked that.

And his mom was wonderful and supportive, just an awesome woman, and he adored her. I saw that, and it resonated with me. Attraction kicked in.

Anthony wasn't a jerk. He wasn't out partying with people. He was going to college, he was going to work, and he was getting out to the clubs every night. He was working hard, and he was exhausted. Of course he was. So my reality was totally distorted. I was what you could call a concrete thinker, and I would project my issues onto others. Before I'd even talked to Anthony, I'd brought my baggage. That's a powerful illustration of how you can get in your own way instead of letting an organic relationship develop.

Anthony would tell me about his magic tricks, how he'd wanted to be a magician known as "the Great Griffini." I thought that was so precious. He was just a sweet, sweet guy. He would open doors for me. He still does. He gets up when I come to the table.

His mother raised a really awesome kid. And I thought, *If he adores me the way he adores his mother, I have a good chance to be happy with him.*

3

Living in Black and White

I enjoy being married, but there's one tip I'll give any man thinking of marriage in the near future: When it's time to buy the ring, whatever you do, go alone. Because if you take your lady, I guarantee you not even Disney World will have anything that compares to the ride you'll be going on that day.

Anthony

I proposed to Brigitte in a Chinese restaurant in Hyde Park. It was a fancy place, in a penthouse, and Brigitte was enjoying the meal so much that I was like, *Man, how am I ever going to get in the question?* I don't remember whether I went down on one knee, but I was serious. I was nervous, as most men are.

Her response was, "I'll think about it."

What? That's not the kind of response you see in the movies. There's no "I'll think about it." It's "Yes, of course." I was more confused than upset.

Brigitte excused herself to go to the bathroom. She was crying and had to compose herself.

Brigitte

Anthony figured out early in our courtship that I was a foodie, so on this night he took me to an Asian restaurant atop a historic high-rise building; this place had linen tablecloths and napkins and crystal stemware. Nice. As usual, Anthony encouraged me to order anything I liked, and back then I could put some food away. Anthony always watched in apparent amazement while I ate, yet this time he seemed mildly distant as if he were preoccupied or nervous. But I was too busy gettin' my grub on to think too much about it.

Eventually I came up for air, and Anthony and I casually chatted—but I guess I was still anticipating the next course because after the waiter left our table, I could have sworn I heard Anthony say "marry," "love," and "life." I looked up, and Anthony's eyes were welled up with tears as he tried to suppress what I've come to refer to as his "chronic ugly cry"—that look someone gets when he's using every facial muscle to avoid crying and ends up appearing to have some rare neurological disorder. That's the image I recall of Anthony that night.

To confirm that I hadn't imagined what I'd heard, I asked, "Wha' chew say, Tony?"

"I want you to marry me," he answered in a quivering soft voice. "Will you marry me?"

For the first time that night, I swallowed but didn't taste my food. Before I could edit my words, I said, "Tony, I gotta think about it," and I left the table.

Yep, I said, "I gotta think about it." Who says that? How idiotic. As I fled to the ladies' room, I must have been holding my breath because once inside I let out the loudest whoosh of air, which came with a flood of tears. The other women in there asked whether I was okay, but I couldn't catch my breath to answer.

One woman started rubbing my back while another held my hand and said, "Chil', you okay. What's goin' on?"

"Girl, what he doooo?" asked another one.

Eventually I explained, and in unison they harmonized, "Aww. Congratulations, baby!"

They spent a moment helping me get my face together, and I returned to the table, apologized to Tony, and explained to him that it was a lot for my brain to take in.

Anthony

After dinner we sat in the parking lot, and she asked about my plans. I told her I'd be going into the entertainment business and performing, and I laid out what that would take. It would be hard at first, but that was what I wanted to do.

We talked about it for a while, and before the evening was over, she said yes.

I hadn't yet bought a ring when I proposed. I was working as a bellman and had maybe $600 in my pocket. So I took her ring shopping, and when we entered the store, I went right, and she went left. Right then I should've known I was in trouble. Brigitte was talking to the jeweler and came up with a marquise-cut diamond. See, and I thought all diamonds were round. It was like buying a car; you walk in thinking you're going to get *this* car, and the dealer winds up selling you *that* car. Her ring was so expensive that the jeweler gave me mine for free.

Brigitte and I were married June 28, 1986, at Merrill Avenue Baptist Church on the Far South Side, a block from where my parents lived. I was in a white suit while Brigitte wore a cream-colored dress.

Brigitte

My wedding dress was a custom-made, two-piece number in an off-white silk satin. My main design inspirations were the art deco sophistication of artist Erté and the '80s fashion genius of designer Norma Kamali. Patti LaBelle and Grace Jones were my wedding dress muses. Patti rocked that look the best.

The bottom layer was a simple tank-top dress, with a cinched-in waist and a fishtail train. The top piece included long dolman, also known as batwing, sleeves. The waist length of the top narrowed at my midthigh. The neckline was high, just above the collarbone. Pearl embellishments adorned both sleeves and the collar. The shoulders included that '80s padding and pearled embellishments that dropped down and narrowed to a tassel of small pearl beads, stopping midtriceps.

Anthony

White, Irish, Jewish, and gay friends from college and work came to the wedding, which confused my stepfather. He came up to me and said, "Some white people are in the back of the church. You know them?"

"Yeah, Dad."

In his world that mix of people didn't happen. Our generation was different.

Brigitte and I lived in Rogers Park, and the North Side was like a separate city from the South Side. When you lived on the South Side, you didn't go north. Yet there were so many things to do near my new home. In our building were a dry cleaner and a bank, with nearby supermarkets (a rarity on the South Side) and restaurants, including our favorite hangout, Barry's Spot on Broadway. On the South Side you needed a car because the public transportation options were so limited. On the North Side, express buses would take you downtown, and the "L" was two blocks away.

The most challenging period of our marriage was probably those first few years when you're making two people into one. When we were dating and went to McDonald's, I'd have fries, and she'd have fries, and that was that. Then we got married, and my fries became her fries.

"But you said you didn't want any," I'd say.

"Yeah, but I'm still taking some."

The little things would add up, even stupid stuff, like whether the toilet paper should hang over or under the roll. (Over, of course.)

It's a matter of learning to trust the other person. We said "I love you," but I didn't fully trust yet. Brigitte probably did, but it took me a while. She'd say, "I'm with you. I'm for you. When I ask you where you've been, it's not because I'm trying to trip you up. I really want to know where you've been in case something happens and you need help, or I need help."

These conflicts, of course, eventually worked themselves into my material:

I've discovered the worst thing you can do to your wife is keep a secret from her—because if she finds out from somebody else first, there will be hell to pay. I learned that the first time I worked overtime and didn't tell my wife. As soon as I walked in the door:

"How come you didn't tell me you had to work overtime? How come I gotta find out from somebody else first you gotta work overtime? I bet if I was Janet Jackson you would have told me you had to work overtime!"

"Hey, if you were Janet Jackson, I wouldn't be working."

I tell her everything now. I don't care how small it is either. "Honey, I'm about to clip my big toenail now. Is that all right with you?"

"Why you telling me?"

"Because I don't want you to find out from anybody else first."

Our schedules at that time were out of sync. She was still working nine to five at the Park Hyatt while I was performing at night and beginning to make a name for myself. One day the owner of Zanies called to ask, "Would you like to open up for Jay Leno?"

"Yes, yes," I replied.

The gig was at the Zanies in Nashville, so I needed the week off, and I got into a big fight over it with my supervisor at the Park Hyatt. I threatened to quit because I was going to become a big star. He finally relented: "Okay, take the week off."

I called back the Zanies owner within ten minutes and told him I'd had a big showdown with my boss but got the time off.

"Oh, we got somebody else."

That was my awakening to how the entertainment business operated.

Soon I quit the hotel, and my workdays began at night. I wasn't bringing in much money, so a lot of the financial burden fell on Brigitte. I was committed to becoming an entertainer, trying to find my place in a comedy world where not everything was black and white.

Back then the Chicago-area comedy clubs, such as Zanies and the Comedy Cottage, were part of the white world. Such clubs didn't exist in the black world. Other black comics and I learned our craft in dance halls, nightclubs, lounges, and other places where people drank, smoked, and cussed, and guys were trying to push up to women.

When comedy was at its peak in the '80s, it seemed like every establishment was featuring it, even if nine out of ten places weren't well suited for it. Hotels, restaurants—everyone thought it was easy: just hire some people to tell jokes.

I performed everywhere and figured out what made people laugh. I didn't know what my style was, so I tried everything. Friends tell me now, "You were corny; you were goofy." I *was* goofy and corny. I was twenty-one. I didn't know anything about life. I wasn't drinking. I wasn't cussing. The one time I tried cussing onstage, somebody said, "Just go back to doing what you're doing, Griff, because you don't sound right cussing."

Some places might have strippers on Monday, comics on Tuesday, and bowling on Wednesday. I would hit the stage after strippers named Chocolate and Black Licorice. They were picking up dollars and quarters with their butt cheeks, and now . . . *Here's Anthony, the comic who doesn't cuss or drink!* I was out of my element.

I impersonated Mr. T selling Avon and Stevie Wonder doing a Visine commercial. I made a Michael Jackson kit with the glove and a hair band. It was stupid—like Jimmy Fallon kind of stupid. But he became host of *The Tonight Show*, so stupid can get you all the way to the top.

Yet some folks thought that, if anything, my approach was highbrow. "Oh, Anthony, you're just telling jokes," the brothers would say. "You're trying to be smart. You're trying to be sophisticated. You're trying to be white."

"No, I'm trying to be me."

That attitude drove me crazy. There are thirty million blacks in America, and we don't all eat fried chicken, and we don't all live in the city. Lumping everyone together has been detrimental to blacks because we don't appreciate that we're very diverse. Yet we hear that if we talk correctly, we're trying to be white. If we don't listen to hip-hop, we're not really black.

In the black comedy world of the 1980s, everyone's goal was to be the next Richard Pryor or Eddie Murphy. I wasn't like either of those guys.

It was hard for me to find my audience, and that was depressing. I wanted to give back to the community, but the community thought I was square. The brothers wanted you to be black, and I thought I *was* black, but they wanted you to be a specific black.

So those black club audiences wouldn't listen to me. Why pay attention to this kid trying to tell this stupid joke when you could look at the stripper going onstage? That world was not mine. I would blush and call a stripper "ma'am." She's in front of me, topless, and I'm looking down. I was that guy. I couldn't look at her. It was against how I was brought up. No one taught me about the world of Chocolate and Black Licorice.

Yet out of that world came one of my best friends in the business, Bernie Mac.

I met him at one of the nightclubs when we were both starting out. The same comics would see each other over and over as we tried to get our three to five minutes onstage. He was another comic looking for exposure, and we formed a bond.

If we were jazz musicians, Bernie was Louis Armstrong. You knew he was coming. I was more Charlie Parker; if you listen, you will enjoy it, but I'm not going to blow real loud. I can't sustain that. I've been quiet all my life. Bernie was a raunchy comic in the tradition of Redd Foxx, Richard Pryor, and Dolemite (the pimp persona of Rudy Ray Moore).

Bernie thrived in those strip joints and lounges filled with people drinking, smoking, and cussing. He blasted through everything. He played the black route, the street route, the "Chitlin' Circuit" route. He and I would perform at places like the Godfather Lounge, Chic Rick's, and the Copper Box, and he'd grab your attention no matter what you were doing.

But he couldn't break into the white clubs because they didn't get him. Those audiences didn't understand where he came from.

Not that Bernie cared. He wasn't going to change his style for anyone. Early on he and I did a show at a church, and he was cussing and telling the raunchiest stories, paying no attention to the audience's shocked expressions. He was Bernie, take him or leave him.

I wasn't as fearless as Bernie, but I could go back and forth between the white clubs and the black lounges. I've always been a crossover comic because my style of comedy can appeal to anybody. Working both worlds helped me develop my craft—and get on television.

While I worked the clubs, I got used to dealing with hecklers. These were guys who thought they were funnier than you, three or four of them who usually rode together. A guy didn't heckle you if he was on a date, but guys with other guys, they'd been drinking, and they thought they're part of the show. I still had the advantage though. I was a professional comic. And I had the mic.

I might go up to them and say, "Here, you take the mic. You're funny." Suddenly the lights were on them.

"No, I'm good," they'd say.

I had to be careful, though, because some brothers are funny. They'd wait in the audience, like counterpunchers, for me to say something they could attack to get some laughs. Usually I could defeat them as well.

"Wow. You must've just gotten out of prison. Do you need a hug?" was one line I'd use.

Or if someone shouted something that truly was funny, I'd say, "Aw, I'm going to use that tomorrow. Thank you." That's how you take their power.

I didn't get heckled *that* often, but when it got really obnoxious, I wondered, *Why are you stopping me from doing my job? People paid good money to hear me, not you and your boys.* I never understood that and still don't. Sometimes other audience members would take on the hecklers: "Come on, man. I paid thirty bucks. Shut up."

I learned that the worst heckler is a drunk woman. If it's a drunk guy, you can shut him down with the audience on your side: "Get him! Get him!" But if it's a drunk woman, people think of their mom or sister, and you can go only so far before the audience turns on you. The worst was having a bachelorette party sitting right up front, making a lot of noise and not listening to you. There was really nothing you could do.

These experiences helped prepare me for my years in Hollywood in one key way: I became immune to rejection. It started in college when I auditioned for parts that went to the blond-haired guy. On the stand-up stage, rejection was a near constant. *They don't like me? They don't like this show? They're not paying attention? Don't worry; another joke is coming.* That's how I thought about it.

Fear of rejection can be an obstacle to growth. When you're starting out, you don't know what *not* to say. You're talking about anything and everything. You may not really know how to put a story or joke together. Now I can look back and say I know how to construct and deliver that joke; I know how to talk about this and that. In the beginning your creativity is like a shotgun, spraying everywhere, and it takes practice to hone your skills and become more accurate.

Brigitte

The first time I saw Anthony perform was at the Star Plaza Theatre in Merrillville, Indiana, and it was exciting. I said to myself, "My goodness. He looks really good under those lights. Whoever lit him, lit him very well."

He was tall, he was handsome, and I wanted to tell everybody in the audience, "That's my man! That's my man!"

He was very funny. He was clean, and I was used to blue humor. He was corny as hell. But he made me laugh.

I was less in tune with what he was saying and more in tune with how everyone else was responding. That became more and more the case each time I saw him perform. I mouthed his routine from my seat because I heard him rehearsing so often that I knew where every beat was going to land, when every pause for applause was going to come. One time while he was telling a joke, I breathed in deep and didn't exhale until the audience laughed. I realized I had held my breath for about ten seconds without even thinking about it.

As I sat there, I felt obligated to help Anthony and the audience. I made a point of laughing when they were supposed to laugh. Sometimes Anthony's humor was sarcastic, and I didn't know whether the audience got it, so I helped them out with a precursor laugh—because laughter is infectious. Then I would do the studio clap.

There's a difference between a studio clap and a regular clap. A regular clap is "Wow! That was great." A studio clap is faster, more rhythmic. That's how they teach you if you ever go to a sitcom taping. It sounds different on tape from a regular clap, which comes out sounding kind of lazy in comparison. When you do the studio clap, the person next to you starts clapping with that rapid, rhythmic pace too.

I was working so hard in the audience, I eventually said, "I can't do this anymore. I have to be backstage." It was so exhausting. When Anthony would point me out in the audience, or they would find out who I was, they would look at me reacting to him. They would check whether I was laughing before they would laugh. Afterward they would ask me if it was true that I did those crazy things that Anthony had said onstage.

"Oh, that's so funny!" they'd say.

Nah, I didn't need all that. I'm an introvert, so I would prefer not to be seen, not be heard. It became rare for me to sit in the audience. It was too stressful. Generally I stood in the back or on the side or by the stage so when Anthony would come off, I'd be there.

Or I stayed in the greenroom.

Or I stayed home.

Anthony

While I was pushing my comedy career forward, I was also auditioning for acting roles in town. The first dramatic role I landed was for an ABC series called *Jack and Mike*, which aired from September 1986 through March 1987. Shelley Hack, formerly of *Charlie's Angels*, played a newspaper columnist for the *Chicago Mirror*, and in my episode, called "Personal Foul," she's investigating how a functionally illiterate high school basketball player—that was me—keeps getting a pass from his coach and teachers so he can play.

"Hey, you're going to ruin my career and my life," I said.

"Yes, but don't you understand? You need to get your education."

"My education is playing ball. I don't need school because I got skills."

That wasn't the actual dialogue, but you get the idea. There was never an episode like that about a white kid.

I was also cast in a TV movie, *The Father Clements Story*, that aired on NBC in December 1987. It starred Louis Gossett Jr. as a real-life Chicago priest and Malcolm-Jamal Warner (of *The Cosby Show*) as the troubled teen he adopts. I played a kid who bullies Warner.

I enjoyed those experiences, but after I graduated college, I devoted most of my time and energy to stand-up. I was performing a lot in town and also hit the road. Two other comics and I became a mini troupe, driving around in a little motor home as we did a touring version of the TV game show *Make Me Laugh*. We'd arrive at a college during the day, promote the show on campus, and then perform at night. We'd do our regular stand-up sets first, then let the kids be contestants. If we didn't make them laugh, we paid them $25 each, which was like $1 million on campus.

We hit 175 colleges in one year. We drove eight to twelve hours, did the gig, and then drove another eight to twelve hours for the next gig. We had to drive twenty-two hours to hit one spot in Michigan's Upper Peninsula. It was wintertime and snowing. We'd have no time to set up or to rehearse—or to sleep, for that matter.

"We can't do a twenty-two-hour drive in twenty-four hours," we told the booker.

"You gotta do it; you gotta do it," he insisted.

During a particularly windy part of the drive, I crashed the motor home into a snowbank, damaging the vehicle and flustering the three of us. But we made it to the venue on time and performed the show.

Sometimes the circumstances were ridiculous. Once I was performing at a hotel in Kenosha, Wisconsin, and an Elvis impersonator was on the bill. For some reason he had bodyguards. There was no greenroom or dressing room, so we were all changing our clothes in the hotel bathroom, with Elvis's bodyguards crammed in there with us.

I thought I was a big baller because I was just out of college making $500 a week and seeing the country. Meanwhile, Brigitte was in Chicago with a baby on the way. We'd been married for less than a year when she became pregnant, and she was having a rough time of it. She couldn't keep anything down and lost a lot of weight. She was also anemic.

I was performing at the club Barrel of Laughs in Oak Lawn, a suburb southwest of Chicago, when she called me in between sets. Her threshold for pain is pretty hard-core, so she was far along by the time she told me, "I think the baby is coming."

"Hey, I gotta go," I told the club owner.

I sped home, picked Brigitte up, and took her to St. Joseph Hospital on Chicago's North Side. By the time we got there, the baby was ready to come out. We had set up this whole pregnancy plan and paid for a birthing room, but when we mentioned it at the hospital, the nurses said, "No, that's not gonna happen."

Before her doctor could get there, Brigitte gave birth in the emergency room. As I'd later say onstage:

The labor only took thirty minutes. It was unbelievable. It was like giving birth to a Domino's pizza.

It was November 8, 1987. The baby hadn't been due for another month. Our baby girl was underweight, about five pounds. When I told my mom the news, she said, "Look: you were a preemie. You were underweight. You didn't walk until you were like twelve or fourteen months old."

We named our daughter Brittany, a combination of Brigitte and Anthony. Her full name was Brittany Nicole Griffin, and her nickname was Nicky. I would call her Nick Nick. Brigitte would call her Brit Brit.

While taking Lamaze classes with Brigitte, I learned that an unborn child can hear you from inside the womb. So I talked and sang to Brittany before she was born, and when I spoke to her right afterward, she immediately turned to me as if she recognized my voice. That was an amazing moment.

Aside from her early arrival, there was another complication. The doctor pulled us aside to tell us that Brittany had Down syndrome. I didn't even know what that was.

"Just love her," my mom told me, "and we'll see what happens."

4

Moving Up and Out

My daughter was extremely small at birth. The biggest
baby at birth on record, believe it or not, is a twenty-two-
pound baby boy. Women, if you ever have a boy that
comes into this world at twenty-two pounds, don't buy
him any toys. Buy him a work permit.

Brigitte

Brittany's disposition as a baby was one of pure delight. Her affect was mostly
cheerful. She was just a sweet, sweet baby—good eye contact, reciprocal communication, an ability to imitate, a love for playing peekaboo. I would take
her for my retail therapy to Marshall Field's department store every Sunday. I
just loved it.

I think she had my spirit in that if she didn't want to do something, if she
was very resistant or stubborn, she didn't do it. But she wasn't a crabby baby.
She was multidimensional in her personality. She loved it when I would talk to
her. In the kitchen I would say, "I'm going to throw these carrots away; don't
tell Daddy," and she would give me a look as though she understood. She had
a great sense of humor. She loved to laugh, loved to giggle.

I had left my job at the Park Hyatt shortly after Anthony and I got married, and I worked at Ravenswood Hospital as communications manager up

until Brittany was born. I stayed home with her for several months. Then I had trouble leaving her to go back to work. Finally, I got a great job as a customer service representative for MCI on Michigan Avenue.

Sometimes I'd arrive home late from work, and Anthony would say, "I just put her to bed. Don't go in there and have a conversation with her."

So, of course, I'd go into her room and start telling her about my day, and she'd coo and giggle. Then Anthony would come in and complain, "Now she won't be able to get to sleep."

But I was just a mother missing her child for eight hours in a day. I'd been waiting with bated breath to get home so we could hang out. She loved for me to read to her. She was really receptive to the verbal stuff, and she responded to extreme facial expressions, which I loved and which was consistent with her dad being a goofball.

Brittany was, oh my goodness, just awesome. She smelled baby fresh. Sometimes when she was in my lap, I just looked at her fingers and the folds in her hands and the fat folds on her legs. Sometimes I would gaze into her eyes and get lost, and she would start giggling. I felt so warm gazing into her innocent, clear eyes and then at her gummy smile. When her first couple of teeth grew in, they were spread out. And she'd jabber and babble like she was having a conversation. She was mimicking what she overheard. She was a very easy baby, never tensed up when somebody held her. She was very receptive.

I loved being around her. She gave me energy that coursed through my veins. I was so enmeshed with her that I couldn't distinguish where she ended and I began. We were completely synchronized.

Anthony

Brittany's scalp was tender, like mine, and I was the one who combed her hair. If there was no moisturizer, then it didn't get done that day. If I tried to comb it without moisturizer, man, she would scream.

Usually, though, Brittany was happy, and I was happy. She was like me. She had my temperament, just chilled out. I don't really freak out over stuff, and that was true of her too. Brigitte said she was like a little Tony.

Brittany shared my love of laughter. She was a late walker but could beat you on all fours to the door. She would just row, row, row. I saw her get stronger. I saw a lot of things first—like when she pulled herself up in her crib—because Brigitte was working during the day, and I was with her.

She didn't seem developmentally slow to me because she was our only child; there weren't other kids to whom I was comparing her. She was one of the family, along for the ride.

On some nights when Brigitte was working and the sitter either was late or couldn't make it, I took Brittany to the clubs with me. I'd ask the waitstaff to watch her while I performed; she was easy. Sometimes I even brought her onstage, and if she was asleep, I pointed her face toward the wall. Then I delivered my set. If she woke up and started making noise, that's when I told the audience good night.

I hated leaving her and Brigitte when I performed out of town. Comedy club owners put you up in horrible places where they would never stay themselves. One time in Dallas, I noted to the club owner that the condo didn't have a TV or other amenities.

"This is a crack neighborhood," he said. "The TV was stolen. So was some other stuff."

Before I went to bed that night, I put a dresser against the door so it couldn't be opened. That was the drill in numerous places: I'd block the door with a dresser or jam a chair under the knob.

In Atlanta I was put up at what I thought was a regular hotel, but when I checked in, the desk clerk said, "Don't come out of your room after ten." Sure enough, at 10:03 I heard shouting and fighting and cries of "I told you to give me my money!"—followed by gunshots and people running down the hall. Because I was nervous that someone would burst in on me while I was in bed, I did that thing you see in gangster films: I stuffed pillows under the covers to make it look like someone was there, and I slept in the closet.

When I came out the next day, I learned that my "hotel" was a halfway house, which was why the comedy club owner got a good discount for putting up his performers there. Over the next couple of nights, though, I still did my shows at the club and returned to that room. Where else was I going to go? I didn't have the money to stay at another hotel.

You go along with it because you don't know how to complain, and there's always a comic who will be willing to stay there if you don't.

Usually three comics were grouped in one of these condos: the headliner stayed in one room, the middle-of-the-bill guy stayed in another, and the opener slept on the couch up front. When I had the choice, I'd pick the room farthest in the back, explaining to my condo mates, "If a burglar or thief comes in, I'll hear you guys cry, and I can get out the window."

At that age I was so naive about life, I thought, *Okay. I guess this is how it's supposed to be.* None of the other comics were complaining. We all were trying to get somewhere, and because we were all in it together, we didn't realize how bad it was.

When Brigitte joined me on the road with Brittany, though, she noticed.

Brigitte

I didn't like the way Anthony was treated on the road. It was a hazing process. I think it was very abusive the way club owners treated comics.

The final straw for me came when we were in Milwaukee with Brittany. That I was with my child was what got me most upset. It was the dead of winter, and the club owner put us up in what they called a condo but was really a studio apartment with a separate kitchen. The apartment was in a lovely old building across the street from a grocery store, but the unit itself was unkempt. Anthony and I slept on a pullout sofa, and we had a crib for Brittany. There was no telephone and absolutely no heat. I regret even saying this, but we turned up the oven and opened the door to heat the room.

Back then buildings didn't have carbon monoxide detectors, and in this studio apartment, the windows were painted shut and sweating; we couldn't open them to let out some of the gases. We all could have wound up in heaven together.

"I can't do this anymore," I told Anthony. "If you can't speak up for us, then I'm going to advocate for my child."

It was scary for me that we had to resort to opening an oven door for heat instead of going to a hotel. It was horrific. That's the word I choose: *horrific.* It wasn't like war-torn Bosnia, but as an example of someone being exploited and mistreated, it was terrible.

Back then Anthony wasn't willing to stand up, and it was difficult for me not to get involved. That's where fractures in relationships sometimes occur, because if the performer handles his business in a certain way and the spouse sees that he may be taken advantage of, it's difficult not to speak up. I knew if I would have lobbied for my way of doing things, Anthony probably would have given in, but at the same time, that could have created more resentment between the two of us. I might have gotten my way but at the expense of his ability to get work because, back then, the more receptive you were to being mistreated, the more the club owners wanted to book you.

Anthony

I was growing as a comedian, and my work was becoming more personal. I'd gotten married at twenty-three, so I would talk about that, and after Brittany was born, I riffed on having a child and the effects on a marriage.

I worked everywhere I could: weddings, birthday parties, bowling alleys, cruise ships, bars, the grand openings of restaurants, and private parties in people's homes. You do all you can to learn your craft and to find out who you are and what your voice sounds like.

The key is to reach that next level, where you can speak about what is happening with you and make it funny. Earlier comics, such as Henny Youngman and Bob Hope, just told jokes, and they left me cold. Jerry Seinfeld was a good observationist, but I didn't feel like I knew anything about him, so he rarely made me laugh. What made a performer compelling to me was peeling back that outer layer to reveal someone interesting underneath.

I also was learning what makes different audiences laugh: men, women, whites, blacks, older folks, younger people, and so on. When you go on tour, you also find out which areas of the country may not be receptive to black comics (or black people, for that matter).

I was on the road with three other comics down South on Martin Luther King Jr. Day, which hadn't been a holiday for that long, and we stopped for gas.

"If we'd killed four more, we'd have the whole week off," the gas station attendant said.

I wasn't scared though. This was a part of life. Chicago is a big city, and you knew where the bigots lived, so it was nothing I'd never heard before. In one of the white clubs in Chicago's suburbs, one guy said to me after my set, "Hey, let me buy you a drink. You were funny. You've got to understand that no one here likes you."

Sometimes these people treated me as an exception, like Bill Cosby back when he was so popular, like I wasn't really black. I just rolled with it and moved forward.

When you're starting as a comic, being booed is not the worst thing. The worst thing is people not paying attention to you. You have no control when they don't see or hear you and instead go about their business until the headliner comes out. The way some of the bills were put together, the deck was stacked against you from the start.

For instance, I was standing in front of a curtain before a rock band came on. I didn't even get the whole stage, just the apron. As I performed, I heard the band tuning their instruments behind the curtain. Could the audience hear that too? I didn't know. If they could, I might make a joke about it. But if not, I'd risk them saying, "What are you talking about?"

The lesson? Ignore the extraneous stuff and do your show.

The Chicago comedy scene got a boost when the Improv, an offshoot of Budd Friedman's groundbreaking New York comedy club (and its younger cousin in Hollywood), opened in a bustling part of downtown by Michael Jordan's Restaurant. The Chicago Improv was taking aim at Zanies and Funny Farm, the town's top comedy clubs at the time. Its co-owner and president was Walter Gertz, the father of actress Jami Gertz, and he was very supportive of me.

Soon after the Chicago Improv opened, it hosted a regional section of the national Johnnie Walker Comedy Competition that Friedman was presenting. Comics from all over the Chicago area and the Midwest came to compete. You had to audition early in the day to get on at night, and a lot of people showed up. My audition went well, and I made it to the stage that evening.

The Chicago Improv was a big room with a capacity of more than three hundred, which was more than double the size of Zanies. Budd and Walter had done a great job with the publicity, so on the night of the competition, the place was packed, and the audience was loud.

Performing there with such high stakes was nerve-racking; my previous biggest gig had been in Merrillville, Indiana. But I'm good at hiding my nervousness. I get so deep into my own head—I've got this joke and must say it this way—that I don't have time to think about everything that might freak me out.

Brigitte stayed at home. She's not good at hiding her nervousness.

In my few minutes onstage, I did Mr. T jokes—he was really popular then—and a bit about Ed Debevic's, a popular 1950s-style diner where the waitstaff would insult you. I said that because the restaurant was set in the '50s, when I would come in, they'd make me work in the back. I also drew on my experiences at the Popeyes at Devon and Broadway to complain about fast-food restaurants:

> I have to wait thirty minutes for my food because the employees are always eating the food they're supposed to be serving. Every time I walk in, they're picking their teeth: "May I help you?"
> "Yeah, I need a three-piece dinner."
> "That'll be about thirty minutes."
> "What about the chicken behind you?"
> "Oh, that's mine."
> And they're always trying to sell their personal belongings: "Would you like an apple pie with that?"
> "No."
> "How about a TV? I've got a nice TV in the back you might want to check out."

I was telling jokes and stories, and that was it. I didn't see all of the other performers, but prop comics were big back then, so I was up against guys who could juggle or play guitar or whatever. At that time, I feared comics who had props because people seemed to love them. Those performers are showing off skills that not everyone has while some folks feel like, *Hey, anybody can tell a joke.*

On the night of the competition, though, when the votes were tallied for my jokes and stories, I won. A few weeks later I headed to the Hollywood Improv to compete in the finals against all of the other regional winners from around the country. Again, I didn't pay much attention to my competition. I just put my head down and did what I'd been training to do.

I'd developed enough material by then that I could deliver a set without being Chicago-centric. I don't think the competition was any better in LA than it had been in Chicago. They were just other comics. I liked everybody and became friends with one guy, Steve, who became a cartoonist for a major paper. I think he was pissed that he didn't win, but we still got along. That's what I don't like about competitions. Everybody has their style, and there's room for all of us. They're funny. I'm funny.

Nonetheless, I was happy to win the national Johnnie Walker Comedy Competition. The prize was $2,000 in cash, which was a lot of money to me. I also was supposed to receive $5,000 worth of bookings throughout the year, though I don't think I ever got them all. There must have been some fine print that I missed. But the contest still provided a big boost to my career.

Part of the reason was that Budd Friedman was a great guy to have in your corner. He was the face of the Improv and not shy about it. He often wore a suit or jacket when everyone else was in jeans, and his trademark was a monocle that he wore, he said, because he had trouble reading the menu at the New York Improv and was too vain to get glasses.

LA Weekly would later write that Budd "basically invented the modern comedy club."[1] Before he opened the original Improv in Manhattan's Hell's Kitchen neighborhood in 1963, stand-up comedians mostly went up to the Catskills to find an audience because comedy in the big city wasn't really happening.

By the time I met Budd, comedy was booming everywhere. Budd opened a lot of doors—and a lot of clubs, including the Hollywood Improv in 1974. Not only were the clubs nice, but so were the condos where he put up the comics. He knew how to treat people well. Even in Chicago, where I didn't need a condo, the conditions at the Improv were a big step up from what the other clubs were offering.

Budd always liked rubbing elbows with celebrities, and he saw that my star was rising, so he took an interest in me. I appreciated that. He had me perform when he opened an Improv in New Orleans, and when he put an Improv on a cruise ship, Brigitte and I got a nice trip out of the deal. Years later he also invited me to perform at the launch of the Improv he was opening in Puerto Rico, and at one point he and I went jet-skiing, which spawned this joke:

---

1. Adam Gropman, "How Budd Friedman, Founder of the Improv, Basically Invented the Modern Comedy Club," *LA Weekly*, September 21, 2017, http://www.laweekly.com/arts/budd-friedman-founder-of-the-improv-basically-invented-the-modern-comedy-club-8665759.

I got a chance to go jet-skiing for the first time. Actually, I didn't go jet-skiing. My jet ski went jet-skiing. I just paid fifty bucks to have an enema at thirty miles an hour.

When Budd did anything, he did it in style, and he always took his wife, Alix, with him. The two of them catered to Brigitte and me when they didn't have to. They were good friends.

That my career was gaining momentum was confirmed by the call I received from *Star Search*. That show was a big deal, a popular TV talent competition that preceded *American Idol, The Voice, So You Think You Can Dance, America's Got Talent*, and so many others. It aired early Sunday evenings, when families were watching, and the host was Ed McMahon, Johnny Carson's sidekick on *The Tonight Show*. The show had eight categories: most involved singing, but one covered comedy.

Previously I'd sent tapes to the show and gotten no response. Now that I was the Johnnie Walker champion, the show was calling me, asking me to come out to LA to be a contestant. I didn't have an agent or a manager. Having someone to consult would have been helpful. My focus was trying to get from one step to the next, but I didn't have anybody saying, "You should do this. You should sign this contract." I was oblivious.

But I knew enough to tell *Star Search*, "Okay."

Brigitte

Anthony's career was on the rise, but he was on the road a lot, which was difficult as we juggled two careers and a child. One day I took Brittany to an appointment with a social worker, and our regular guy wasn't there, and the guy filling in asked me, "Has anyone ever told you that your daughter qualifies for Social Security?"

We didn't know that. We didn't even consider that a possibility. I thought, if anything, we might receive money that we'd have to give back later. I told him I was hesitant to apply because it felt like aid.

"No, this is not aid," he said. "This is because of your daughter's condition."

By now, Brittany's Down syndrome was becoming very evident to us and others who saw her. In order to confirm her Social Security eligibility, I had to take her to a doctor for an assessment. In terms of bedside manner, this man turned out to be heartless. He examined Brittany and explained that she had an extra chromosome, which I already knew. Then he said matter-of-factly: "Children with this diagnosis, you institutionalize them, as they often have heart problems, develop Alzheimer's at a very early age, or die of leukemia."

As he spoke, it felt like slow motion to me. I stuck on everything he said. I didn't remember anything after that.

Later I did my own research and learned that children with Brittany's type of chromosomal disorder—known as Down syndrome or trisomy 21—are vulnerable to a multitude of medical challenges: heart problems; muscle-tone issues that require early infant occupational or physical therapies; a smaller oral cavity; plus increased risk of early mortality due to Alzheimer's, dementia, or leukemia.

We continued to move forward with our lives and to enjoy all there was to enjoy with our little girl. But that doctor's words hung over us like a dark cloud.

5

Star- and Soul-Searching

I never wanted to be a performer growing up. I wanted
to be a racehorse—simply for the retirement benefits.

Brigitte

The Chicago Improv had an event where everyone was mingling, and I was talking with Walter Gertz, the co-owner. He said, "Anthony's very talented, he's a very nice guy, he's a sincere spirit, and he can go places. Chicago is too small for him, and I think your next step is to relocate to LA. I think he can do this. It's time. He's ready."

How do you respond to something like that? As a spouse, I couldn't say, "Get out of here, Mr. Gertz. You know I'm not ready for that. You better take that dream stuff away from here."

So I was like, "Oh, okay."

I knew that's when the sacrifices would begin.

I didn't want to move. Absolutely not. I didn't think we should do it. I did not want to do it.

Anthony and I didn't fight over this. We weren't the fighting kind. And bottom line, I wanted to support him and his dreams.

I did express some of my sadness—about leaving my family and so forth.

But at the same time, moving to LA would offer me an escape from the torment I was experiencing with my mom.

My mother was, to put it mildly, very difficult from my childhood through my adult years. That's why today I can close my eyes in a room and pick out a person with underlying anger issues.

I grew up as an only child, but when I was in my early twenties, my dad said, "I have to tell you something. You're not the first." When I admitted that I didn't understand what he meant, he told me, "You're not the first, but you were the last." My parents had gotten married in a shotgun wedding when he was eighteen and she was almost seventeen, and they were nineteen and seventeen when I was born. Previously he'd fathered at least two other children.

He was a practicing Muslim. My mom was culturally raised Christian but was not a follower, practitioner, or believer. Nuns and priests educated me from five years old onward. When allowed to choose a high school—a rare moment of empowerment for me—I opted for Aquinas Dominican High School, an all-girls Catholic school in South Shore. So my religious upbringing was a bit confusing.

My interactions with my mother were devoid of humor and humanity. There was no joking, no laughter, no touching, none of that. There wasn't any, "Come on over here, girl, and give me a hug." I was fortunate to receive supplemental support from other family members. They were the ones to say, "I love you," "So long," "See you later," and "Miss you."

I never heard "I love you" from my mom, ever. As a young adult I once attempted to coerce it out of her, ending a phone call with, "Love ya, Ma."

Nothing.

I said it again, imagining that she hadn't heard me the first time: "Okay, love ya, Ma. Talk to you later."

Nothing.

I felt myself regressing, like a kid in a candy aisle, making a last-ditch plea. "Hey, Ma, love you."

Finally, she responded: "Okay. I'll talk to ya later. Bye."

After my parents divorced, my mom and I lived in the South Side's Woodlawn neighborhood, near Sixty-Third Street and Blackstone Avenue, right next door to St. Ceros Elementary School, where I attended kindergarten and first grade. The buildings were so close together that you could wedge yourself between them and climb the walls like Spider-Man.

Our apartment was like the one in Lorraine Hansberry's *A Raisin in the Sun* but without the bedroom. It was a studio apartment with a Murphy bed, which my mom pulled down for herself. I slept in the little nook where the Murphy bed was stored. It was small and cozy. I felt I was escaping the real world to sleep in my own little dollhouse.

My mom was very punitive. When I was in kindergarten, a friend and I crossed this big street, Stony Island Avenue, to get to the pond at Jackson Park. If people saw a five-year-old girl crossing such a big street now, they'd be calling Child Protective Services, but this was an era when you didn't worry about your children being outside, and the people in the neighborhood were like secondary caregivers. Anyway, my friend and I were by the water, and she fell in. She didn't know how to swim, but I could swim like a fish, so I got in and pulled her out.

She had to go home, but I knew I couldn't because my mother would get mad that my clothes were soaking wet. Instead, I spread out in the sun in the middle of Jackson Park, trying to get my clothes dry. I lay facedown so the sun would dry the back of my clothes, and then faceup to get the other side. At that young age, I was so fearful of my mom finding out that I'd gone into the water.

One time when I was in day camp, I was bullied by a girl who said, "Give me your swim cap strap."

"Well, what am I going to wear?" I asked—because when you're black, you don't want to get your hair all puffy. This girl didn't care.

When I got home, my mom said, "Why is your hair all puffy? Where's your swim cap?"

I showed it to her, minus the strap.

"You better have it when you come back tomorrow."

I knew she wasn't kidding. I went back the next day and beat up that girl—because I was thinking about what would happen to me if I had to go home again without a swim cap strap. I was afraid of the girl but more afraid of my mom.

I never let the outside world know what was going on behind our closed doors. As a child I was determined never to betray my mother.

The Blackstone Rangers, a prominent street gang, had a big presence in the neighborhood, but I think that because my mom was known, they kind of protected me. I ran—or at least wandered—away from home a few times, and they always found me and took me back.

When I came home once with an award from a high school forensics competition, my mother didn't acknowledge it. She said something like, "Get that [bleep] out of my face." That's the type of person she was. I looked forward to the out-of-town competitions; they were my refuge. On weekends I tried to stay out of our home as much as possible. I went to my aunt Cookie's house and babysat for other aunts and uncles.

I was seventeen when my mom kicked me out of the house for good. She was on her second or third marriage by then, and this husband was closer to my age than to hers. I don't think she was comfortable with that, though I thought of him more like a brother than anything else. I was just glad to have someone else at home to take the brunt of her anger. He was cool, but he didn't have the backbone to stand up to her.

She had thrown me out several times before, and I'd stayed with my grandparents or my aunt. Every time I got kicked out, I said to them, "Please don't let me go back; I don't want to go back." Being away from home was liberation. It was like the tethers had been cut.

But I always went back.

Before this final incident I had packed my red backpack, just in case, because I'm always trying to be one step ahead. But I wasn't prepared to be thrown out of the house the way my mom did it. I was coming up the stairs one day when she met me on the landing, swore at me, and ordered me out. My bags and my books were in my closet ready to go, but she stood in front of me and wouldn't let me pass. "You know what I'll do if I have to tell you again," she said.

I knew she kept a gun in a Seagram's Crown Royal bag in her bedroom. I took her seriously. As I was headed out the door, she said, "And don't go to Mother's house."

I had been so indoctrinated to do what she said to do that I didn't call my grandmother, which I easily could've done. I didn't even call my dad. I didn't call anybody those first few weeks. This was during the summer, so we were out of school. I lived on the streets. I didn't do drugs, I didn't prostitute myself—let's get that off the table right now. I sofa-hopped, and at the time I had a boyfriend who was in college, so I slept in his car for a while.

When I told my dad about all this later, he said, "Why didn't you call me?"

The answer was the same reason he never took action regarding her behavior: fear.

So when my mother told me not to go to my grandma's, I didn't do it. But I did eventually call my aunt from a pay phone and ask, "How's it going?"

"Fine. Where you at?"

"I'm just out."

She knew from the tone in my voice that something was up. She got me to admit that I was calling from a pay phone and the reason, and then she demanded that I get over to her house. I told her no.

"I am not afraid of your mother," she said. "Get over here."

I got on the bus and never went back home. That was one of the most freeing days of my life.

My mother wasn't out of the picture though. She came to our wedding, and when we arrived at the reception, Anthony asked, "What is this?"

We hadn't wanted alcohol at our wedding. Anthony and I didn't drink, my dad hadn't yet gone into recovery (though he would, successfully), and for others, including Anthony's biological father (though he didn't come), drinking was an issue. Yet when we walked into the reception, there was a full-service bar, ordered by my mom.

"Listen, baby," she said, "ain't nobody going to come to no party and not have drinks. We don't do that in our family."

Anthony never says anything negative about anyone, but one day he said to me, "She's not a nice person." Everyone has redeeming qualities as far as Anthony is concerned, so when he said that, I felt validated, really validated. I just broke down and cried.

Anthony

You know that movie *Misery*, in which Kathy Bates terrorizes James Caan? When Brigitte and I saw that, we looked at each other, and I said, "That's your mom."

Brigitte

These behaviors don't come out of nowhere. As I've learned from my mother's siblings, she may have been prone to emotional challenges, given that my grandparents also were late adolescents when they wed and started a family—and my grandmother did not have the benefit of being fully reared by her own mother, who died during my grandmother's youth. After my mother was born, my grandparents had three more children, and my mother had to play a major role in raising them. I recall my mother expressing justifiable resentment about her parentification at a young age. Although her siblings' experience with her as a caregiver was consistent with my own, they would acknowledge to me how difficult it must have been for her to be forced to take on that responsibility with her three siblings.

I am grateful to my mother for one thing in particular: she sparked a passion in me for learning and especially reading. My mother was a voracious reader; she would consume each *Reader's Digest* cover to cover. When she was reading, I felt safe. As a child, I believed that the more I read, the more I could curry favor with her; it would be our point of connection. It never worked that way; our mutual love for books resulted in no expressions of love or admiration from her. But books remain my great escape.

I try not to make comparisons between my mom and Anthony's mom, Sharon, whom I loved. She was less like the mother I never had than the sister I never had. She was a young mom, too, so she was only about ten or eleven years older than me. She was a great mentor and a classy lady. You would never know she was raised in the projects, but you wouldn't be surprised to learn she was a valedictorian. We talked for hours on Sundays, and she was always there for us. Anthony adored his mother, and I could see why, so that endeared her to me even more.

My mother and I kind of reconciled after Brittany was born. I wanted to allow her to see my girl, and she did.

Eventually I was willing to let her watch Brittany for an evening. One time, when Anthony was out of town, my aunt drove me to my mom's house so I could drop off Brittany. I went upstairs, and my mom was sitting in the dark. I think she had been drinking.

"What's going on?" I asked.

"Oh, just drop the baby off and get the [bleep] out of here," she said.

"Uh, no. What's going on?"

"I told you, just drop the baby off and get the [bleep] out of here."

"No, I'm not doing that," I said. "That's not an option."

I never, *ever* talked smart to my mother, never sucked my teeth at my mother, never cursed in front of my mother, and never slammed a door because in a black house you don't slam doors, you don't suck your teeth, and you don't say "What?" So I was being defiant just in saying, "No, I'm not leaving my daughter with you."

One thing led to another, and I said, "Mom, you need help. You really need help. I don't know what's wrong with you."

That infuriated her, and as I was picking up Brittany, she jumped on me. I was saying, "No, don't! Stop, stop!" but she wouldn't let me put Brittany down. I thought if she backed me out of the door, she very likely would push me over the banister with Brittany in my arms.

Eventually I was able to set Brittany down, and for the first time in my life, I fought back. I had been passive all of my life, but now all the rage that had built up for so long came out at once. I gave her two times as much as she gave. And my mother always has been strong as a bull.

It was a matter of life and death. The only reason I responded in that way was because of my daughter. My mom was going back to her room to get the Seagram's Crown Royal bag, so I swooped up Brittany, grabbed the diaper bag, and ran down the stairs and out the door. I started yelling at her from the middle of the street. Never before had I spoken to my mother in this way.

Brittany was crying and screaming as I got into the car.

"What the heck is going on?" my aunt asked.

"I never want to see her again," I said.

So at this crossroads in Anthony's and my life, despite all my misgivings, moving from Chicago to Los Angeles represented a gain for me. I could get away from all of that toxicity. I would miss the rest of my family, but, otherwise, Anthony, Brittany, and I would have a fresh slate in California.

Anthony

While Brigitte and Brittany stayed in Chicago, I flew to LA to scout out a new home. After checking out different neighborhoods, I went to the Valley, where one of my cousins lived, and found a nice two-bedroom apartment. It was just me, my sleeping bag, and no furniture.

While I was out there, I tried to learn more about Hollywood and how to navigate the industry. *Star Search* was coming up.

Back in Chicago, I continued my preparations. We still didn't have much money, so I found a shop on the South Side where I could buy three silk shirts for sixty-nine dollars. Those, plus two pairs of pants (one of which I wore on the plane), were my wardrobe for the trip back out to LA for *Star Search*. If you watch me on the show, you can see that my shirts alternate with each performance while my pants stay the same.

For this show, two comedians would go head-to-head with two-and-a-half-minute sets. I was comfortable with that because I had plenty of material. In a sense, such a short set makes it easier for anyone to win because you need only those two and a half minutes, not a full evening's worth of material. When some of the comedians who won the show's $100,000 prize would perform at clubs later, they'd be required to deliver forty-five-minute- to hour-long sets, yet they might have only five minutes of strong material. A lot of club owners would complain, "We don't like people on *Star Search* because they can't fulfill their obligations." But I was prepared all around.

At *Star Search* you kept performing until you lost. You competed in the morning, and if you won, the next round was in the evening. If you won that one, you returned in the morning, and if you didn't, you got a plane ticket back home.

The crowds for the day's two tapings were entirely different. In the morning senior citizens were bused to the show because those were the people most likely not to be working. In the evening the audience was made up mostly of people in their twenties and thirties. I didn't adjust my performances for each crowd; I wasn't advanced enough to have separate sets of material for different demographics, and I was trying to appeal to everybody anyway. I just told my jokes.

While her grandmother watched Brittany, Brigitte came with me to LA but didn't attend the tapings. They were too nerve-racking for her, so she waited for me in the hotel where the show put us up.

I received little guidance before going in front of the cameras the first time. I was trying to cram everything into my two and a half minutes. Now I look back at the performances and think, *Man, slow down, slow down*. I was scared. I was nervous. This was my first time on national TV, and no one was telling me how to pace myself. I didn't know where the cameras were. Everything was new and a blur.

In my first match I was challenger to the reigning champion, Karen Haber. I riffed on Mike Tyson, the heavyweight boxing champion who had been destroying his opponents:

I'm glad to be out in LA. Last time I was here, I saw Mike Tyson. That's a scary brother; I don't care what anybody says. I personally feel Mike Tyson is nothing more than a pit bull that's been trained to walk on his hind legs to fight. I would never fight Tyson in my life. If I had to choose between fighting Tyson or fighting my mother, I would fight my mother. I'd be in the ring going [throws jab], "Stay down, Momma, stay down. If you get up, I will hit you again."

And that hurts me to say that because I've never hit my mother. I tried to hit my mother one time, and she looked at me and said, "If you ever hit me, that will be the last thing you ever do." And I knew she was dead serious just by the way she cocked that gun to my head [applause].

Tyson's scary. I saw one of his fights where he literally hit this man so hard the blood shot on *my* face. And I'm watching the fight in my living room. He beat this man to the point that after the bout, the loser was asked what his future plans were, and all he could say was, "As far as I'm concerned, Mike Tyson is the greatest fighter of all time. But, hey, you know, don't count me out. I'll be back. I'm just going to take the next year and a half to basically concentrate on, uh, breathing. Then hopefully, with the help of my trainer, we can pursue other matters, such as finding out who am I and which evil spirit possessed me to get into the ring with that man" [applause].

The judges scored the round even, awarding each of us a 3.75 out of 4. So the decision went to an audience secret ballot, and when the votes were tallied, I was the winner.

Even though she lost, Karen Haber turned out to be a good friend and remains one to this day. She held out the olive branch and said, "If there's anything you need, please let me know." She saw how green I was on *Star Search* and painstakingly walked me through the process: what to expect and how to approach the competition. She also helped me get acclimated to LA, both the town and industry. Her husband was working for one of the studios, and they invited Brigitte and me to dinner, and she and Brigitte grew close.

In the second round, I went up against a professional bowler-turned-comic from Jacksonville, Florida. Among other things, I talked about ring shopping for your wife-to-be:

> If women shop with you, they shop for the biggest ring possible. "Well, that's nice, but I was looking for something more crystal ballish."
>
> Men, our first stop is the generic section. "Uh, yeah, I want to see the gold-filled ring for $12.99, please. And I hear there's a discount if I mention *Star Search*."

It all went over well. After I was declared the winner, Ed McMahon said to me, "Congratulations, Anthony. Your second win. How does your wife feel about your routine?"

"Oh, she loves anything that gets me out the house," I replied, drawing laughs.

"We're going to see you next week," McMahon said, shaking my hand. "You'll be out of the house. You'll be right here. Thank you. Good luck."

I won several more times, each victory earning me an oversized $5,000 check printed out on poster board. Brigitte knew how the round went when I slid the big check under the hotel room door.

I was brought back for what they called the semifinals and was pitted against a former medical student named Willie Randolph. My routine included an impersonation of the Reverend Jesse Jackson ("I negotiated for the release of Goldilocks when she was held hostage by the Three Bears . . ."), a bit about wanting to be a racehorse, and a riff about bodybuilding, complete with poses:

> I tried bodybuilding one time, but I believe you can only excel at bodybuilding if you have facial expressions that only come about due to constipation.

My challenger, who had a long mullet, did a high-pitched imitation of someone on a fast-food-restaurant speaker before he picked up a tricked-out electric bass on which he played Bruce Springsteen's "Fire" while the lyrics flashed over the fret board. Yes, he was a prop comic. At the end of this round, our scores were tied, so the audience had to decide by secret ballot. This time I lost.

That, I figured, was the end of *Star Search* for me. Brigitte had already gone home, and it was time for me to join her and Brittany.

Brigitte

We were going to fly back to Chicago together after Anthony lost, but he kept winning each round. I'd be sitting in the hotel room, and all of a sudden, he'd slip this three-foot-by-two-foot $5,000 check under the door.

That was great, but eventually I had to go home to be with my daughter, so I flew there alone. When I got there, my grandmother told me, "Brittany won't eat. She keeps sleeping. She lies down in the middle of the floor. She's lethargic."

Brittany's little hands were orange, jaundiced. She had no energy.

Anthony came home from California but almost immediately went back out on the road. Meanwhile, I took Brittany to the pediatrician, and he wasn't telling me what I wanted to hear; he wasn't diagnosing what was going on.

I told Anthony, "We're going to have to fire that bird and take our daughter someplace else." He said we'd go together when he got home.

All of this took place over a matter of days, a week at the most. I picked up Anthony at the airport, and we took Brittany to Children's Hospital.

She didn't come out for months.

6

Patient and Profiled

Every twelve seconds a crime was being committed in the city, which was scary—especially to me because that meant every twelve seconds I was a suspect.

Anthony

As soon as we got to the hospital, the doctor looked at Brittany and said, "How long has she been orange? She needs blood right away." He told us that her platelets were so low that if we hadn't acted right when we had, she might've gone to sleep and never woken up.

Brittany, who was close to two years old, didn't understand any of this, of course, and wasn't about to lie still to take a needle. She had to be strapped down to the bed, which only irritated her more. She was crying. She was screaming. They couldn't give her a shot because she was so upset.

We had to calm her down and soothe her because she was looking at us, her protectors, like, *Why are you letting this happen to me?*

You could see it in her eyes. It was painful to watch.

Brigitte

The doctors gave Brittany a blood transfusion, but her heart, which had a hole in it, could not handle such a high volume of blood at once, so she went into cardiac arrest. Within twelve hours of entering the hospital, she was in surgery.

When she woke up, she became very agitated and tried to pull out the nose tubes and IV lines, so by the time I went in to see her in the ICU, the doctors had bound her hands. She had this look on her face, like, *What is going on?*

We still needed to know what had caused Brittany to become so ill. I asked the doctors, and they said, "We're thinking it could be either sickle cell anemia or leukemia."

Naturally I harked back to the doctor who was so blunt in telling me about leukemia. Although I was hoping it was sickle cell, I kind of knew it wasn't.

Yeah, I knew it wasn't.

They ran their tests and quickly made their diagnosis: acute nonlymphocytic leukemia, or ANLL for short. The prognosis was poor.

The doctors wanted to give Brittany chemotherapy, but the treatments would be rough on her because she was so agitated and confused. They recommended that instead of keeping her in restraints to administer the medicine, it would be better for her quality of life to place her into a medically induced coma for the duration of her treatments. We agreed.

She was asleep for about two months.

Anthony

Everything was moving so quickly that we didn't have time to think. Brigitte got medical books so she could understand everything the doctors were saying. They would use a medical term, and she would ask, "What does that mean in layman's terms?" She wasn't going to miss anything.

I told the landlords at our new LA apartment that we couldn't move in because of what was going on. They were very nice about it and returned our security deposit. Yet because we'd been ready to move, we'd given up our apartment in Chicago, so we had no place to stay. It was a blessing that Ronald McDonald House, a charity organization that provides support for families with sick children, was able to put us up for a few months. The chapter was just three blocks away from Children's Hospital, located in Chicago's upscale Lincoln Park neighborhood.

Brittany remained in the intensive care unit the whole time she was asleep.

Only one person at a time was allowed in to see her, except when Brigitte and I went in together. We talked to her and played music for her, including Raffi tapes because she'd enjoyed listening to him. The music was comforting. Our daughter was at Children's Hospital, the best place she could be, and we all were doing what we needed to do. She seemed at peace.

Thank God we had family to provide support. The bills were piling up, and I had to work, but I didn't want to go away until I felt confident that Brigitte was being helped and comforted. Her grandmother came every day, and my mom was there constantly as well. Sometimes you feel God's presence through the love of family members, like my mother. She was a pillar who gave me faith. With family members and friends gathered in the waiting room to surround and protect Brigitte, I thought, *Okay, I can go out on the road and perform and take care of business.*

I traveled a lot and was glad that we still were based in Chicago. This was our home, where we had family and friends and a great hospital. All of these things together would help us get past Brittany's medical crisis.

Brigitte

My maternal grandmother was deeply entrenched in her faith; she was a rock. And Anthony's mom was like the other pillow, so we were cocooned in this biblical support system that would rock you to sleep like a baby. It was phenomenal.

I'd left my job at MCI after we decided to relocate to California. Brittany was in good health then. I would not have resigned my position if I did not have all my ducks in a row.

Everything happened in short order. All of a sudden Brittany had leukemia and was in the ICU in a coma, and we were living at Ronald McDonald House after a brief stay with my mother-in-law. Before all of this happened, I had been on cloud nine—about the move (despite my concerns about leaving our families) and the fact that Anthony was closer to fulfilling his dreams. Then I crashed emotionally. It was too much for me, and Anthony kept going out of town.

Brittany was so peaceful sleeping at the hospital, and as she received her chemotherapy treatments, she was slowly losing her hair. My coworkers from

MCI came to visit, which I really appreciated, and my family was there, too, including my mother. So I had to deal with that.

I kept forgiving my mom, always, always. She would come to the hospital, and I thought she would help, but then she would play these crazy games. I'd be back home in bed, and she'd call me from the hospital and say, "Why aren't you here? Why are you at the Ronald McDonald House?"

"Mom, I'm sleeping. I've been there since five in the morning."

"You should be here," she'd say. "You should always be here at nighttime because that's when the nurses hurt babies."

One time when I needed a respite and some company, my mom told me, "Oh, go ahead. I'll watch the baby." I thought that was really nice of her to allow me to go to lunch, to visit with friends. But when I came back, a dark look was on her face, and there was that silence I'd experienced so many times.

"What happened?" I said. "What did I do this time?"

She swore at me.

"Okay, but when I left about two hours ago, you were fine," I said.

"Don't keep asking me no questions."

"I'm not asking you a question, I'm just making a statement."

"Don't even talk to me."

I thought right then and there, I'm just going to play it safe, be a diplomat, and when I finally get on that plane to California, that will be it.

And it was. After I boarded that plane, I never spoke with her again.

Anthony

When I was a teenager, I got used to being pulled over by police for no reason. In Chicago, you always had incidents. It was a common practice: If you were black, police pulled you over and wanted to know what you were doing. If you drove a car and saw police do a U-turn, you knew they were coming for you. When I was going to college, I would have friends in the car, and we'd see a cop car and say, "Yeah, they're gonna stop us." Sure enough, the next thing we heard was "Get out; put your hands against the car."

When I'd go into a department store, the security guard would watch me, and I'd notice a woman clutching her purse a little higher. It was interesting to me because I'm always quiet, but I observe what's going on.

My brother, Danny, became the first black cop in the suburb of Park Ridge, and he got a call to look for an assailant. Then another call came saying to watch out for a black guy dressed like an officer.

"That's me," he said.

When I was in high school, police officers swarmed me at a bus stop and accused me of attempted murder. They hauled me off to a hospital to the bedside of a man who had been stabbed.

"Is this the guy?" one officer asked.

"No," the stab victim said.

"Okay, you can go," the cops told me.

I was at the hospital with no way to get home; the cops weren't about to help me, and my parents didn't know where I was. But I was grateful that that was my biggest problem. If the victim had answered yes and then died, I'd probably still be in prison right now.

That was not my final experience with racial profiling.

Brigitte

Late one night—it must've been about 1:00 a.m.—Anthony and I were leaving Brittany at the hospital and walking back to Ronald McDonald House. It had been a long day, and we were joking around on the sidewalk.

"I'm going to get you, Tony," I said.

The light at the intersection ahead of us was changing. "I'm gonna run to the light," he said.

"Hurry up," I said.

"I don't want to run too far because I'll probably get stopped by police."

I laughed. "You're silly. Go get the light."

So he was running, and I was trying to catch up with him, and sure enough, a police car did a U-turn and started flashing its lights. When the officers reached Tony, they stopped and shone their lights on him. One officer had his hand on his gun, and the other one got out of the car. He had a wide-legged stance, like he was ready for trouble.

When I caught up to them, the police were already asking him questions: "Where are you coming from? Let me see your ID. Where are you going?"

That's when I went off.

"What is going on, Tony?"

He didn't say anything, just gave me a look, like, *I told you so.*

"What's going on?" I asked the officer.

"Well, there was an incident in the neighborhood," he said.

"Okay, we didn't just come from 'the neighborhood,'" I said. "We just came from the hospital. Our daughter is in a coma, and she has leukemia. I don't know what's going on. Do we look like criminals? Does he look like a criminal? I don't understand what this 'incident' has to do with us leaving our daughter, who is in the ICU, and going back to the Ronald McDonald House."

"Ma'am, we just got a call, there was an incident in the neighborhood, and he fit the description." The officer kept repeating that.

"Well, what *was* the description?" I asked. "Help me understand, just in case I see the guy."

Finally, the officer couldn't take any more. He claimed they'd gotten another call and had to go.

"Well, okay," I said as he fled. "If I see the person that looked like my husband, I'll let you know."

Anthony

I felt sorry for the officer.

Brigitte

They probably would have hauled Anthony off in a squad car if I hadn't shown up. That stuck with me for a long time because I didn't see Anthony as someone who would fit a profile. I knew him as a sweet guy who didn't have a mean bone in his body. I never wanted to believe what my uncle and my dad always told me, but it was true. They said that you had to have two languages on display when you walk the streets of Chicago, depending on who you're encountering. You have to be very stealthy about how you interact with authority figures because they can misinterpret your behavior as aggression. It's too bad, it's sad, and it's not fair, but you have to be bilingual with your body language.

I didn't fully understand that until I experienced it. Then I started worrying about Anthony. There was this level of angst that I would always feel when he was away. Back then we didn't have cell phones, so whenever he was late or wouldn't call on time, I would hark back to that night.

It changed me. It definitely changed me.

Anthony

I wasn't mad. I was exhausted because of what was going on with Brittany and everything else. I was trying to support my wife and daughter while I tried to keep my career going and pay the bills. This was just one more thing.

In the meantime there was good news on the career front. I'd assumed that when I finally lost on *Star Search*, I was done. But I'd won so many times that the show invited me back to compete in the finals. By coincidence I'd be going up against another black comic from Chicago, Michael Colyar. I knew him from home, though he'd been living and working in Los Angeles for a while and understood the business way better than I did.

I still didn't know what I didn't know, but I'd done pretty well so far.

Although tough challenges lay ahead, I was optimistic all around.

7

Rising Stars

It's very expensive out here in California. I went shopping for some gym shoes the other day. Came across the Reeboks that advertise "the Pump." They cost $175. Now, I feel if I'm going to pay $175 for some basketball shoes, those shoes should be able to play basketball without me. I should be able to drop them off at the gym, pick them up later, and ask, "Did we win?"

Brigitte

After Brittany's chemotherapy treatments had been completed, the doctors told us that if her vital signs and platelet levels were good, they would bring her out of her coma. I wanted to be as emotionally and intellectually prepared as possible, so I asked the nurse to describe what this process would look like, and she walked me through it.

This wasn't a Dorothy-waking-up-after-her-adventures-in-Oz sort of scenario. It was a more gradual progression as the doctors slowly weaned my daughter off the medicine that had kept her asleep for about two months.

We kept everything consistent. We still played music for her and spoke to her, all softly. She had her blankie there, as well as one of her favorite stuffed animals, Tweety Bird. All of those familiar, comforting items were around her when she came out of the coma.

Before they woke her up, the doctors gave Brittany a tracheotomy. They had waited to do this until they were sure she was out of the woods. They said that giving her a trach at that point was prudent because if she had woken up with tubes in her nose, they would have had to restrain her again to prevent her from pulling them out.

When I entered the ICU one morning, Brittany's eyes were half-lidded, and she was semi-alert. Another morning I came in, and she was awake.

I was elated, but I looked at it analytically. That's how I'd been taking care of myself emotionally: I'd been trying to take myself out of the maternal role and put myself into the role of a nurse. I had to compartmentalize that way for my sanity. Now that Brittany was awake, I allowed myself to take appetizer bites of joy, just little samples. Wear it for a while, enjoy it, and if I felt emotionally safe, I would open myself up more and enjoy the moment. One might say I wasn't fully emotionally present, but that's how I prepared myself.

Anthony

Brittany was groggy at first but soon was herself again. Her mommy and daddy were there, and she definitely knew who we were. She was babbling as infants babble. I don't think she had any idea of what she'd been through and for how long.

We felt such relief—that she was with us again and that this ordeal had passed. It was a joyful, intimate moment for our young family.

The doctors moved her out of the ICU and into her own room. Soon the doctors had more good news: she was in remission. Eventually she was able to leave the hospital, and we all stayed at Ronald McDonald House while her immune system built back up.

This relatively quiet period allowed me to travel back to Los Angeles to find another apartment to establish roots for us in North Hollywood. Unlike in Chicago, LA apartments didn't come with refrigerators, so I found a used one and also visited thrift shops and other secondhand places to furnish the place. That was the first time and last time that a woman had no say in what I picked out for a home.

The next phase of our lives was beginning at last.

Brigitte

We loosely use the word *remission*, but it's a relative term when it comes to pediatric leukemia. Technically speaking, you're considered in full remission when you've been cancer free for four to five years. But when you're dealing with a child who has had Brittany's type of leukemia, you're looking at her blood cells and hoping her platelets are up to a certain level. After Brittany's platelets remained stable for two months with no evidence of cancer, she was considered to be in remission—or partial remission, at least.

Before we could take Brittany out of the hospital and back to Ronald McDonald House, Anthony and I had to become really adept at all of these medical procedures—some that every parent should know, such as CPR, and some that no parent should have the need to know. Brittany had to have her blood tested so frequently that instead of repeatedly sticking needles into her arms, the doctors surgically installed a line into her vein with a port coming out of her chest. One of our jobs was to keep that clean.

The transition to Ronald McDonald House was gradual: first we took her there for a few hours a day and then for a few days. The doctors remained concerned that her immune system might become compromised.

But eventually she was able to stay with us there, and not long after that, the doctor gave us the go-ahead to travel by plane. I wasn't relaxed about any of this—I never would be. But I was eager to move on.

It was time.

Anthony

Once we had the green light to travel, everything happened fast. We packed up as much stuff as could fit in our Honda Accord, and a comedian friend and I drove it to California while Brigitte and Brittany flew. We all met at the new apartment.

We felt like—*boom*—we got through this and now were moving forward.

And I was in the *Star Search* finals.

I think even more people saw me on *Star Search* than on *The Tonight Show*. When *The Tonight Show* was on, kids were in bed while other people were getting ready for work the next day. The Sunday evening slot for *Star*

Search made it family viewing, especially at a time when cable TV had yet to catch on and most people tuned in to a handful of channels.

Later, when I went to swap meets or stores, people would look at me, and I always thought maybe I knew them from somewhere.

"No, dummy," Brigitte said. "You've been on TV."

I had an aunt in Chicago, no longer with us, who was living on the streets. She would yell, "I got a nephew on *Star Search*!" She would shout it at the rooftops.

A childhood friend happened to be at a bus stop one time when she was doing this, so he called me up asking whether I knew this woman. At first I was quiet because we didn't talk about her; she was one of those black sheep you didn't mention outside the family.

"Yeah, why?" I finally said.

"Because she's on the street, stopping traffic and yelling, 'I got a nephew on *Star Search*, all y'all! And his name is Tony Griffin!'"

She was my street team.

Vying to be named Best New Star 1990 in the comedy division, I was going up against Michael Colyar. He was a street performer who would tell jokes on Venice Beach and bring in thousands of dollars. To see each other again in Hollywood and be together in the *Star Search* finals was cool. It didn't feel like competition to me. It was, "Hey, I'm going to do my stuff, you're going to do your stuff, and the judges are going to pick."

Michael was way ahead of me in terms of management and having things together. He had consultants and assistants. I had me. He was a seasoned performer and still is very funny. In the black world people know him; in the white world, not so much.

Though he and I were friendly, Michael wasn't messing around. He was into mind games, like putting posters on his dressing room door that said, as I remember it, stuff like, "Big Sheriff in Town," "I'm the Last Man Standing," "Get Out of Dodge." He wore a dark hat and an outfit made especially for the show: a jean jacket showing Wile E. Coyote with broad orange, yellow, and brown stripes stretching across the shoulders and chest.

I wore a yellow dress shirt buttoned to the collar, plus a brown vest. I performed my set at a speedy clip, as if I were trying to land as many jokes as possible in that short time. I reprised the ring-shopping bit and talked about how my family never had enough money when I was growing up:

My brother always had to wear my hand-me-downs. He never had anything new. Even his childhood pictures were old pictures of me [applause]. It's true. My father would tell him, "Danny, this is you in eighth grade."

"I'm not in eighth grade yet."

"Well, this is what you gonna look like in eighth grade. And take a good look because these are the clothes you'll be wearing."

I also joked about having a dog:

People say dogs will lay down their lives for you. That's a lie. I had a fire in my house last year; my dog was the first one out of the house. In fact, I didn't know there was a fire until he called me up on a pay phone across the street. I'm running outside going, "Hey, man, why didn't you bark?"

"Hey, you got a smoke alarm. I heard it."

My set went over well and felt good. Michael came out and did a "black check," explaining, "If there's not at least three blacks in the audience, I don't work. I'm sorry. It's in the contract, ladies and gentlemen."

In his raspy voice, he then declared, "The subject tonight is racism," and he proceeded to tell jokebook jokes about different ethnic groups. Mexicans, he said, "got their own phone company, Taco Bell." He made fun of Jheri curls: "What kind of grown black man wants his hair to look like Shirley Temple?" And he said that as a half-Jewish/half-black child, "I was confused. I didn't know whether to steal it or buy it wholesale."

As I listened, I thought I'd win because my material was original.

He ended his set by announcing,

Ladies and gentlemen, I joke about racism because racism is a joke. Every man is your brother. We are not separate from each other. Even the guys who call themselves skinheads, they're your brothers too. Sure, they're confused Nazis with a bad haircut, but they're still your brothers, and I say this to you: take some time to be kind to your brother and kind to yourself, and may the hand of God be with us all [blows a kiss]. Good night.

I rolled my eyes at this, but when the people in the audience applauded enthusiastically, I thought, *Uh-oh.*

He knew the game.

After we finished our sets, Ed McMahon asked each of us, "If you win the $100,000, what will you do with the money?"

I said I would help my mama out.

Booo!

Okay, nobody booed, but it was like, *That's it? You want to help your mama?*

Yes, doesn't everybody?

Michael Colyar said he'd give half of the money to the homeless, and he received another big round of applause. In the greenroom afterward, everyone was going up to him and saying, "What you said was so meaningful."

There were tears in people's eyes. That's when it dawned on me.

I was toast.

Brigitte

Nowadays Anthony and I talk about how everybody on *The Voice* or *American Idol* or *The X Factor* has a human-interest story. Either they're fighting cancer or overcoming other great odds in some way. You can't get on the show with just your talent.

When Anthony first was on *Star Search*, our daughter was struggling with Down syndrome, and when he went back for the finals, she'd been diagnosed with leukemia and had spent two months in a coma. Anthony didn't have a team with him to say, "Listen: that's a human-interest story. If you know that Ed McMahon always asks the finalists what they would do with this money, perhaps you could be prepared to share something about Brittany."

Instead, Anthony said, "I'm going to buy my mama a house." That's a stereotypical black person's answer, even though it was sincere and heartfelt. When Michael Colyar said he was going to donate half of his money to charity, that's Human Interest 101. That made the judges think, *Ah, he has substance.*

I've never regretted that Anthony didn't use our daughter's illness to boost his career. But that is the sort of thing that helps on TV competition shows.

Anthony

Before they announced the winner, we were told, "You're going to stand there, and if you lose, smile with grace."

We came out and stood side by side, and Ed McMahon said, "The $100,000 grand comedy champion . . . Michael Colyar."

As he took his bows, Ed McMahon shook my hand and said, "Good luck in your career."

Losing on *Star Search*, I was in good company. Martin Lawrence, Dave Chappelle, Drew Carey, Rosie O'Donnell, Ray Romano, Kevin James, Adam Sandler, and Dennis Miller—as well as Justin Timberlake, Britney Spears, Christina Aguilera, and even a group featuring Beyoncé—all performed on the show without winning the championship. Dennis Miller lost his round to Sinbad, who also went down in the finals. Someone who actually did win the $100,000 comedy prize was Brad Garrett of *Everybody Loves Raymond*.

Still, I was shocked that I lost. Because the show was taped in advance, I couldn't tell anyone the outcome, so I kept my mouth shut.

One good thing about the delay between the taping and airing was that I could watch the shows at home with Brigitte and Brittany and see how confused my daughter got as she looked back and forth between her daddy on TV and her daddy sitting right next to her.

Up to that point I'd been getting a lot of calls from agents and managers asking for meetings with me. But as soon as I lost—I mean, *as soon as I lost*—I couldn't get any calls returned. No one tells you they won't return your calls. No one says, "It's not like Chicago; they won't listen to you in Hollywood." These people want to make money, and if you can't convince them they can make money with you, they can make money without you.

When I called people seeking representation or jobs, I always got the secretary saying, "He's not in. Would you like to leave a message?" And I never heard back.

Eventually Brigitte, who always has been more intuitive than I was, said, "Honey, they got your message. Did you get theirs?"

8

Road to 'Tonight'

I have one uncle; he has fo' teeth, all of them gold. Fo',
not four. Fo'. Four is when they're all together.

Anthony

Even though I had lost *Star Search*, two of the judges had told me, "Don't
worry. This is just a TV talent show. You have staying power."

At the time I didn't get it. When you're young, you're thinking, *I sure
could have used that money*. But I joked onstage that I was okay with losing *Star
Search* because I didn't want the hundred grand to ruin me.

Still, a career is a marathon. There's so much you don't know in your
twenties—about your work, about life—so the key is to keep developing. One
casting director said he wished he could tell people not to come to Hollywood
till they're thirty—but Hollywood makes its money off of people who are in
their twenties, when they're handsome and pretty but don't necessarily know
their craft.

The truth was that *Star Search* had given me great exposure, and in
Hollywood that translated to work. Everyone in the business knew who was
on TV, how well they'd performed, and how they'd been received. Plus, I was
in tight with Budd Friedman, who owned the Hollywood Improv, where I'd

won his Johnnie Walker competition. Budd was larger than life, and if he liked you, he really liked you.

Being booked at the Improv was a coup because all of the comics were trying to get in there or the Comedy Store, both of which were packed every night. Those were the two LA clubs that broke the most comics, places where you'd be seen by TV shows' talent coordinators and others who could help your career. Talent coordinators were the town's gatekeepers, and the clubs had gatekeepers in front of gatekeepers.

I could never get into the Comedy Store because I wasn't owner Mitzi Shore's type of comic. Richard Pryor and Eddie Murphy were; you could be as blue (risqué) as you wanted at the Store. You could be blue at the Improv, too, but the trajectory was different. The Store had Jim Carrey, who was wild and goofy. In general, the Improv was more for monologuists. I was an Improv comic.

I was fortunate to get to perform there, which led to appearances on *An Evening at the Improv*, Budd Friedman's series on the A&E cable network. The show was taped at the Chicago and Hollywood clubs, and in one episode, Mr. T introduced me and then laughed in the audience as I impersonated him:

> I grew up in Chicago a couple blocks from Mr. T, and I can remember a time when he had only one gold chain and a mood ring to his name. In fact, he used to sell Avon cosmetics. Can you picture that? . . .
>
> "I'm a real man, an Avon man. I pity the fool that don't buy Avon!"

As in Chicago, I was playing as many places as I could. I worked gigs at the Ice House Comedy Club in Pasadena and the Laugh Factory in Hollywood, which was smaller than the Improv and Comedy Store but home to the Fox Network's *Comic Strip Live* stand-up series, on which I appeared.

I also played the black clubs where whites wouldn't perform because they were in black neighborhoods. These places were like Chicago's lounges, though some, such as the Comedy Act Theater in the Crenshaw neighborhood, were more established. That's where Robin Harris, another comic originally from Chicago, made his name.

In a black club, you wanted to go on first or second because we all had similar material: we grew up poor in the inner city and had crazy mamas and dads and drunk uncles. If you were the sixth comic on that night, the first five had already told your life.

Too many black artists were putting themselves into a box and were fearful of being ostracized if they tried to step out of it. Many black comics modeled themselves after whoever was big, so everybody was cussing like Richard Pryor and talking and dressing like Eddie Murphy, who, in his hit stand-up movie *Raw*, was wearing all leather, including the gloves.

We all talked about being black. That's what was expected, yet I began to break out when I started talking about life *aside from* being black. I was trying to be different from everybody else, and the people in the black clubs thought, *Man, this dude is boring.*

For me the important part was that I was working and learning. My busy schedule paid off when, after one of my Improv sets, a casual-looking guy in his late fifties approached me and said, "I like what you're doing."

I thanked him, and he asked whether I lived in LA. I told him I'd recently moved to town. He put me in touch with his assistant, who was about my age and with whom I would bond. The man asked me to let him know when I'd be performing next and said he'd keep tabs on me. If I had any questions about the entertainment business, I should ask. He wanted to help.

This was Buddy Morra, one of Hollywood's biggest talent managers. In New York he was partners with Jack Rollins and Charles H. Joffe, perhaps best known for managing Woody Allen and producing his films. After relocating to Los Angeles, he continued to work with big-name clients, such as Billy Crystal, Robin Williams, and David Letterman. The fact that he was taking an interest in me was a big deal, though at first, he was so low-key that I didn't realize he was courting me. He opened up Hollywood to me.

Buddy came off as a regular guy, his mellow energy in sync with mine. He was so laid-back that when Billy Crystal and David Letterman talked about him on TV, Letterman referred to him as "the master of the standing nap." He was almost like Clint Eastwood in that he had enormous power but was quiet about it. Many agents announced themselves as agents by the flashy suits they wore and the way they carried themselves. Buddy was nothing like that. I saw him maybe once in a suit. This was *The Cosby Show* era, so sweaters were in, and his assistants wore jeans or shorts and gym shoes because they took their cues from Buddy. He was always approachable, always unassuming. People who have a lot of power don't need to show that they have power.

He invited me to his office on the 20th Century Fox lot. I'm Chicago through and through, so I was never in awe of stuff, but it was very cool to say at the gate, "I'm here for Buddy Morra," and be waved onto the lot.

He became my manager, but that arrangement, too, was informal. He never sat down with me and said, "Here's a plan to get from A to B to C." He also didn't take 15 percent from the get-go.

"You work on your craft," he said. "I know it's hard to live in California, so when I tap you for commission, it will be because you don't feel it."

Buddy was playing the long game and wouldn't accept my money until I was comfortable enough that his fee wouldn't affect me. His aim, like mine, was to get me to that point of comfort.

He came out to see me perform and said I was funny and likable—in the Bill Cosby mold, back when that was considered a good thing—which was what talent coordinators were looking for. After one of my sets at the Improv, Buddy introduced me to another casually dressed, laid-back guy, this one in his late forties.

"I want you to meet this friend of mine, Jim McCawley," Buddy said.

"You were funny," Buddy's friend told me. "I'd like you on the show."

The show was *The Tonight Show Starring Johnny Carson*, and as I soon learned, McCawley was its renowned talent coordinator. When he entered a club, everyone thought, *Oh man, Jim's here.* He could change the world for comics. He had a lot of power—because *The Tonight Show* was *it*.

I didn't know about Jim McCawley or his power, and that probably worked in my favor. One good thing about my manager was he never told me who was in the room or who was watching me, so I wouldn't get nervous. Now I had *The Tonight Show* talent coordinator inviting me onto the show.

"That's great," I said.

What else was I going to say? If *The Tonight Show* wanted me on, I'd be there the next day.

I'd come out to California to do stand-up. I wasn't thinking about sitcoms. I wasn't thinking about movies. I wanted only to perform comedy on a stage, and the biggest stage was *The Tonight Show*. I didn't have a plan for twenty years out, ten years out, five years out. I had one goal, and suddenly there it was, right in front of my face.

Buddy, however, *did* have a plan. He took Jim off to the side, and they chatted.

Although Jim would have booked me right away, Buddy told me, "I'm not going to let you on the show until you're ready to do five shows, in case Johnny likes you so much that he asks you back the next day."

When Steven Wright was on *The Tonight Show* for the first time, he was so different and had people laughing so much that Johnny had him return to the show within a week.

Still, I didn't understand. *What do you mean I've got to wait?* I had to wrap my mind around that because it was confusing to me, a guy in his twenties who thought he was ready to take his shot.

I knew nothing. I would have been really green, and I think Johnny would have seen that.

One thing I liked about Simon Cowell on *American Idol* was that he was up-front with people. He would say, "I've been in this business for twenty-five years, and you're not ready; you're not strong enough; you don't sing as well as you think." Paula Abdul didn't want to hurt people's feelings because artists are fragile anyway. They've been told no for so long that they start believing no. Some of the noes will tear down your armor. But some can be helpful.

Buddy was saying to me, *You're not ready, but I'm going to help you get stronger.* There were a lot of great comics, so I had to step up my game. I was going to be swimming in a different pond. He had a way, the Buddy way, to get me to the next level.

"Let me surround you with people who have been on *The Tonight Show*," he said.

These people would be on the stage and in the greenroom of the Comedy & Magic Club down in Hermosa Beach.

So would I.

But as seemed to be happening all too often, this great news was counterbalanced by bad news. Within days of my being invited to perform on *The Tonight Show*, Brittany, who was showing no symptoms of any problems, had a routine checkup, and the doctors discovered that her cancer had returned.

Brigitte

I wasn't surprised. I had braced myself for this probability. We knew what a recurrence of cancer would look like: the platelets would be low, and our baby would show certain signs. I kept a color-coded journal of the meds they gave her, the frequency of those meds, and the doses. Because I had this copious log and we were so well informed, I already kind of knew what was happening by the time the doctors formally diagnosed her. This wasn't a shock, like it had been in Chicago. She would have to undergo more chemo.

I was conservative when it came to Brittany's care. At the slightest sign that anything might be wrong, I would always call the doctors and take her to Children's Hospital Los Angeles. I didn't deal with the emergency room; I went right up to the unit, where they'd put her in an isolation room and run tests.

In dealing with all of this, I used the tools I had developed as a child who was hyperaware of her mother's mood dysregulations. Accustomed to walking on eggshells and being prepared, I made a point of never being caught off guard. That sense of control has been a survival skill for me. I didn't want the doctors to sneak up on me with information. I wanted to be aware and well informed. I wanted to know every doctor, every nurse who was on call, anybody who was coming in to do anything for Brittany. If someone came in whom I didn't know, I gave him or her the once-over: "Have you seen her before? Have you read her chart? Let's go over it together." I wouldn't let anyone touch her until I was comfortable.

One time a really sick boy was brought to the other side of Brittany's room; he was vomiting, and a nurse was taking care of him. Then the nurse came over to check Brittany's line, but I didn't hear her wash her hands first.

Brittany, who was really antsy, sat in my lap, and the nurse said, "I can't check her vitals until you put her down on the bed."

"I'm not putting her down till you wash your hands," I said.

I had to advocate for my daughter, always.

Anthony

We felt no panic or despair at this point. Though we'd hoped and prayed that Brittany wouldn't relapse—or that at least it wouldn't happen so soon—we knew that this was a possibility. The way I looked at it was we'd beaten it in Chicago, and we'd beat it in Los Angeles too. In Chicago we'd been blindsided by Brittany's diagnosis. This time we were aware of what we were fighting. We knew more now than we did then, and we were out in front of this. We had our team of doctors. We were all together.

Daytime was family time as we managed Brittany and learned all there was to know to let her live at home comfortably. She received her chemo treatments as an outpatient, and because this was a cancer recurrence, the doses had to be stronger than before. Brittany lost her hair again.

To take care of her at home, we had to know how to perform CPR, administer her medicine, work her heart monitor, and measure her vital signs. I was blessed to have Brigitte at my side because while I was preoccupied with preparing for *The Tonight Show*, she took charge of most aspects of Brittany's care. There was so much to learn.

Because Brittany couldn't speak, we taught her sign language. Her hearing was fine, though, and she had a healthy appetite. McDonald's fries were tops on her list, and at home whenever I went into the kitchen, she'd find me there. She knew kitchen meant "eat," and she was always pointing her finger at her mouth.

"Give me a second," I'd say. "I gotta fix the food."

After eating she would sign, "More."

"No, all done."

She would eat until she fell asleep.

We still didn't have much furniture in our two-bedroom apartment; it was pretty much what I'd crammed into my car in Chicago and bought at the Salvation Army after arriving in LA. We had a small TV and didn't watch it much. Brittany liked to climb onto the couch to join us.

She also liked to lie down with us on the bed and get comfortable. The next thing you knew, her feet were in my face, and her head was on Brigitte's ear. She rolled over on us as if she had no idea that her weight was something we could feel.

When Brittany was up, she was ready to go: *Let's eat; let's get moving.* Brigitte always dressed her up, and she liked wearing her hat. As she sat in her baby seat in the back, she never was like, *It's cold. It's hot. Where are we going?* She was easy.

For one of her birthdays, we took her to Chuck E. Cheese's, which had a pit filled with colorful plastic balls where kids would play. When we put Brittany in there, she just sat and started to sink. It was like the first time I was in a pool's deep end, but she didn't yell or seem concerned as the balls were overtaking her. She was like, *I'm in quicksand. Okay.* She was content, just chillin'. We had to pull her out.

I never remember her being distraught. She didn't call for help for anything. She did cry when we got her ears pierced. She looked at us like, *What are you doing? What did I do?* But that was about it; then she was back to being her mellow self.

Brittany could gibber up a storm to no one in particular. One day I put her in her little chair so I could get dressed, and she babbled for twenty or thirty minutes, like she was holding court. She was in her own world.

To make her laugh, I would blow on her tummy or her neck. That always got her laughing hysterically.

To us she remained a typical kid. She was happy.

During the day, we enjoyed our time together, and at night I left my wife and daughter for the clubs to shape my *Tonight Show* set.

Over the years the Comedy & Magic Club, south of Venice and Manhattan Beach along the ocean, has earned the description "legendary." It's where many comics worked out their material for TV appearances, and it still serves that function today. Back in the late '80s and early '90s, Jerry Seinfield performed there, as well as Garry Shandling, Jimmie Walker, and other heavy hitters. Even though he no longer hosts *The Tonight Show*, Jay Leno continues to appear there regularly on Sunday nights.

If comedy were baseball, the Comedy & Magic Club was the minor leagues, where players prepared for the big show. Sometimes they were seasoned pros refining their swings. Sometimes they were young hopefuls seeking their big breaks. In the audience, scouts—a combination of agents, managers, and talent bookers—took in the action.

You could not cuss onstage at the Comedy & Magic Club, which was good preparation for network television and fine with me as well.

Everybody respected the owner, Mike Lacey. He's a real, real nice guy, the opposite of most club owners. Comics could eat and drink for free and rub shoulders with the elites in the greenroom, its walls decorated with signatures of comics who had performed on the stage just yards away. Almost everyone in the greenroom was a comedian you'd see on TV, and it was no big deal. I couldn't help but think, *Oh, wow.*

I learned a lot from watching the performers at the Comedy & Magic Club, which showcased blacks and whites, women and men, as well as novelty acts—because, after all, *Magic* is in the club's name. These people had their own unique styles. Roseanne Barr was extremely funny as she tackled everyday people's problems without ever seeming like a typical woman talking about typical comedy subjects. Rosie O'Donnell fared well there, too, as did such black comics as George Wallace and Franklyn Ajaye, both of whom performed often on *The Tonight Show.* Ajaye, nicknamed "the Jazz Comedian," might talk about mundane stuff, but he did so in such a cool way that he was unlike anyone else.

Getting to perform at the Comedy & Magic Club was like joining an elite club. I was lucky to have Buddy Morra and now Jim McCawley greasing the skids.

Jim was a quiet, unassuming guy in jeans. Nowadays a lot of people behind the camera want to be known as much as the people in front of the camera, but back then the behind-the-scenes people often were happy remaining behind the scenes. Jim didn't need anyone to know who he was or where he was. He also didn't need for people to be recognizing him constantly and trying to perform for him or to show him their scripts. He quietly slipped in and out.

Jim came out to my club performances and made helpful notes, which he'd give to me after I'd performed. Clubs were one thing, television was another, and the jokes that work in one place don't necessarily work in the other.

When Jerry Seinfeld was on the road, he wasn't thinking about what works in a club; he was practicing his craft before he'd appear on *The Tonight Show* or *Letterman.* A club is a place to work out your material, but you need to know what you're trying to do.

Jim reminded me that on *The Tonight Show,* I'd be performing not just for my neighborhood or my city or Kansas or Vermont or Miami or anywhere else but for a nationwide audience of eighteen million. How do you communicate with so many different kinds of people? A comedian such as George Wallace, an old-school joke-teller who aimed for universality rather than getting into racial specifics, was successful because he was able to make everybody laugh no matter where they were. That, of course, was easier said than done.

For one, you had to stand out and offer something different from everyone else. Talking about your wacky mom might work in a club, but it would come across as cliché on TV. Although Mr. T impressions made people in bars laugh, I wasn't going to do that or my Jesse Jackson or Michael Jackson imitations on *The Tonight Show*.

Jim McCawley gave me gentle guidance throughout. He had the pulse of *The Tonight Show*. He was looking through the eyes of late-night NBC and what would strike the audience—those six hundred people in the studio and the eighteen million at home—as funny (and not offensive). Even when one of my jokes bombed in the club, he said, "No, that's fine"—because he knew it would score on the show. On the flip side, he told me when something that drew laughs in the club would not work with Johnny and his audience.

He never said, "That's not for my show," but instead, "What else would you like to talk about?"

"I want to talk about this," I'd answer.

"What else?" That was his way of editing. He didn't say I couldn't do what I'd intended. He just said, "What else?"

I performed two or three sets a night to find the right combination of jokes for a tight six-minute *Tonight Show* set. I didn't write anything down. I just worked at it and worked at it, trying to make myself strong enough to be able to deliver my dream set of jokes—with Johnny Carson sitting just feet away.

9

The First 'Tonight' Set

Thank you very much. I'm glad to be here tonight. In fact, I'm grateful to be anywhere right now because yesterday I had to perform at a grand opening of a Popeyes Chicken.

Anthony

The day before my *The Tonight Show* debut, someone from the show called me to go over what I might discuss if Johnny asked me to sit on the couch after my routine. That's what every comic wants: the invitation to chat with Johnny. The point of this preinterview was to get interesting tidbits that could be fed to him; this was not a show that left anything to chance.

I said I could talk about being married, being a father, being a comic, being from Chicago, and growing up wanting to be an escape artist. I knew that Johnny had started out as a magician, and I could be funny discussing my experiences with a straitjacket. That was like a monologue I had in my hip pocket.

On the day of the show, July 11, 1990, I was nervous, of course. It didn't help that Budd Friedman kept calling me. He'd been great to me as he took me under his wing and booked me in his clubs, but now he wanted me to talk about the Johnnie Walker competition on *The Tonight Show*, and he was pressing. He thought that having the winner promote it on that stage would give the contest a big boost.

I understood that. I didn't really blame him. But I also didn't want to be promoting anything in my first appearance on *The Tonight Show*. I also didn't want to come across as the winner of a talent competition. I wanted to be seen as a professional comic on the rise. And given that I was about to deliver the most important performance of my young career, I needed to concentrate on nothing other than my set.

I called my manager, Buddy Morra, and said, "Hey, Budd is really bugging me to do this, and I don't want to."

"Okay, no problem. I will tell Budd to lay off," Buddy said. As the manager of Robin Williams, Billy Crystal, and David Letterman, he'd put out bigger fires than this.

The Tonight Show taped in the early evening, and I had to be at the studio two hours early. Just gaining entrance to the huge NBC lot felt like a big deal: getting checked off the list, being escorted in. These were not gates I had ever imagined rising for me.

Brigitte couldn't come with me because she had to take care of Brittany. That's just how it was, no big discussion to be had. She would have been so nervous anyway.

I parked my champagne-colored Crown Vic, that popular cop-car model with ample leg room for my six-foot-four frame, and a young page was waiting at the door to walk me backstage. First stop was my dressing room, where there was a small TV plus a welcome basket of fruit, nuts, candy, fancy cheeses, and crackers. I then was shown the greenroom, where family members, agents, managers, and friends could watch the show along with the other guests. Too bad I didn't bring an entourage.

I visited the makeup room so my skin could be prepared for the TV lights' harsh glare. I could've had my hair done, too, but it was close-cropped and easy to manage, so I was good. If you wanted, though, these people would do everything but put on your clothes for you.

Jim McCawley met me in my dressing room, congratulated me, and thanked me for coming. Having gone to bat for me and signed off on my routine, Jim had skin in the game. He escorted me to where the magic happens: the stage.

As we stepped through the gray curtains from which Johnny and his guests emerged every night, I flashed back to when I was a kid and got to be in the audience for the Chicago-based *Bozo's Circus*. Like most kids in Chicago, I used to watch *Bozo* on television, and those characters (Bozo the Clown, Cooky, Ringmaster Ned) and games (including the Grand Prize Game!) seemed to exist in a big world of their own.

Yet when I sat in the stands inside WGN studios, I was amazed at how tiny the *Bozo* set was. It was almost like a living room. A magician would perform against one wall; then the camera would pan to a game being played beside another wall, and then we'd watch Bozo and Cooky throwing pies or something a few feet away. The performers were smaller than I expected too. That was my introduction to the magic of television.

Now, as I took in the late-night talk-show set, I realized: *The Tonight Show* was *Bozo*.

Jim informed me that after Johnny introduced me, I'd walk through the curtains and up to a star on the floor. This was my spot, with Johnny's desk immediately to my right. To my left was the bandstand, and about five feet in front of the star were the cameras: three right in my face. One would be focused on me, one on Johnny, and one on the band. Ten feet behind the cameras were the stands that held about six hundred people, all on top of one another. I had to adjust my approach to performing comedy in this setting because in a club I could be intimate with the audience, but here, those big cameras stood between me and the people. Fortunately, I'd already had a similar experience on *Star Search*.

A mic dangled above my head.

"There's no need to yell," Jim said. "The sound will pick you up. The mic is your friend."

He pointed to where the cue-card guy would stand in case I forgot my material. I've never been able to look at cue cards; I'm always so nervous. And I already have all the jokes in my head because I've been rehearsing over and over and over and over. If the cue-card guy was naked for my entire set, I wouldn't notice.

As we wrapped up, I confirmed with Jim what my last joke would be, and he told me that when my set was finished, to look over at Johnny.

"If he waves you over, you sit on the couch," Jim said. If not, I'd keep standing on the star and enjoy the applause while Johnny said, "We'll be right back," and the show went to a commercial. Then I'd be led back through the curtain for my return to the real world.

Jim and I took a dark walk back to my dressing room, where Buddy Morra was waiting for me. Jim and Buddy knew each other, of course, and were familiar with the situation, so the two of them worked to calm my nerves. Buddy made sure to talk about anything but my routine. Instead, it was "What are you wearing?" and "How's Brigitte?"

I hadn't told Buddy or Jim about Brittany's illness. They'd never met her and knew nothing about her or what Brigitte and I had been going through. I shared very little about my personal life. I played my cards close to my chest and continued to do so for quite some time.

So Buddy, Jim, and I were just shooting the breeze as I changed into a dark shirt and gold-yellow vest. Vests were very in at the time.

I still felt jittery and kept going over the set in my head. I didn't want to sound stupid. I didn't want to embarrass my family.

It wasn't just about them.

Not a lot of black comedians got to be on TV, and I wasn't seeing many black folks around *The Tonight Show*. Most of those I did see were unionized brothers on the tech crew. As I was escorted around the studio, some of them would see me and give me that nod of *Hey, don't embarrass us.* They didn't say that, but that was the look. I think that's the sentiment of just about any minority group: *Hey, don't mess it up for everybody.* So that was my number one fear: *Whatever I do, don't make a mistake.* This applied to what I said, how I dressed, everything.

I wasn't thinking, *Am I going to be funny?* I was thinking, *Just don't mess up.*

There was another knock on the door. It was Budd Friedman.

Oh.

Right away he was asking me, "Are you going to talk about the Johnnie Walker contest?"

Fortunately, Buddy swooped in to distract Budd. Then came another knock, and the door opened to reveal Ed McMahon. This was a nice surprise.

"Hey, Anthony. Great to see you again," he said, shaking my hand.

That made me feel good. I was glad he remembered me.

Budd approached Ed and, gesturing toward me, said, "He came in second on *Star Search*, but he won my contest."

Ed looked at him like, *Who are you, again?* It wasn't a dismissal, but it was a dismissal.

I needed to clear my head and get some private time before my set. Buddy led Budd out the door, Ed departed to get ready for the show, and Jim McCawley left the room as well. Finally, it was just me.

Out on the stage Doc Severinsen's band was practicing while the audience got settled. Side note: every time the show cut to commercials, the band would start jamming, and they were *so good*.

The warm-up guy came out to pump up the crowd. Excitement was in the air. People had come from all over the country to see the one and only *The Tonight Show*. A young comic would be performing for the first time, and Johnny was going to mention that. *Maybe he'll turn out to be somebody*, people were probably thinking, and they could say they saw him back when.

Everything was simpatico.

My mind was thinking of so many things, making so many calculations. I was like a boxer preparing for a fight all by myself. I wasn't taping my hands, but I was checking my clothes, checking my makeup, running through my set in my head.

The band kicked in to the show's famous theme, followed by Ed McMahon's "Heeeere's Johnny!" The audience was cheering as Johnny Carson came out to deliver his monologue. People laughed, the band played, and as I watched on my little dressing room TV, I saw my name appear on the screen and heard "comic making his first appearance on *The Tonight Show*." Everything was popping. I was shadowboxing. I had on the robe. I was ready.

Dana Carvey was the first guest, but I have no memory of his segment or even of his being there. Country singer Travis Tritt, whom I didn't know at all, also was on the show. I do remember the knock on the door.

Showtime.

A young guy walked me the twenty-five or so yards from my dressing room, through a black curtain, and into the backstage area. It was eerily quiet. Now I stood alone behind the curtain that separated me from the stage.

The show returned from a commercial, and I heard Johnny:

Here's a young man making his very first appearance on *The Tonight Show*. He's a stand-up comedian from Chicago [some applause]. He was a finalist, I believe this year, on Ed's show, *Star Search*. He works regularly at the Improv clubs, and he's going to be at Zanies in Chicago, July twenty-fourth through the twenty-ninth. Would you welcome, please, Anthony Griffin. Anthony!

The curtains opened, and I stepped out to the star. Six hundred people were looking at me, plus everyone who would see me through those camera lenses. Johnny was watching. The band was watching. The pressure was overwhelming, but my nerves always register in my hands, not my face. A sense of calm washed over me because I was doing what I came to do.

I remember nothing.

Except . . .

Johnny was close enough that I could hear his laughter. Ed McMahon's, too, and that of Doc Severinsen and the musicians. I could hear laughter from the audience. I didn't hear anything from the camera operators; they were busy. But I definitely heard laughs and applause breaks. I received six of them.

I started out joking about how I'd been performing at a Popeyes Chicken the previous day:

> You know how embarrassing it is to perform at a fast-food restaurant?
>
> "All right, coming up to the mic right now is a very funny brother. He makes his debut on *The Tonight Show* tomorrow, but he's at Popeyes tonight. Please put your greasy hands together for Mr.– Wait a minute, brother. Welcome to Popeyes, sir, may I take your order, please?"

I told a refined version of the bit I'd used in the *Star Search* finals about my younger brother's childhood pictures being old pictures of me. And I drew on marriage and parenthood for this story, also polished after previous tellings:

> Family's very important to me. I'm a father myself. I think the biggest ordeal of having children is the pregnancy. My wife went

through so many mood changes. One minute she would say things like, "Honey, I love you. You're so special. You're my Rock of Gibraltar." And the next minute she would shout, "How the hell can I sleep if you're going to keep on breathing?!"

That's exactly what she told me. She couldn't sleep because she could hear me constantly intaking air. And the week before the labor, she could hear me blink.

I said, "Baby, the only way I'm not blinking is if I'm dead."

And she looked at me and said, "Yeah, so what's your point?"

In fact, I was sleeping one night, and I felt the room become stuffy. Come to find out why was because a pillow had been placed over my head. With Velcro.

After an applause break, I continued:

I was fortunate to be at the labor. I took Lamaze classes, which worked great during the labor itself because while she was screaming in pain, I was in the corner going [breathes in and out], "Hey, that *does* work. You okay, baby? Can you hear me breathe now? I don't see what the problem is."

I joked about how extremely small my daughter was at birth before I discussed babies at the other end of the spectrum:

I have a nephew that came into this world at sixteen pounds; never touched baby food in his life. Went from his mother's breast to a porterhouse steak. He's two years old, drives a truck. "Gotta make that money, baby."

I did my bit about ring shopping for your wife, ending it this way:

My wife picked out a ring that cost $5,000, and I bought it too. I said, "Honey, I love you, and because this is your special day, I'll buy you the ring. But for five grand, when you die, you can bet that ring will not go with you to the afterlife. I don't care if they seal the coffin shut. I'll be paying my last respects with a blowtorch in my hand."

I closed my set with a story I'd been refining for a while:

The biggest responsibility a man faces once being married is that he must protect his spouse no matter what the cost. Someone tries to stick up your lady, fellas, you must shield her with your body. And, women, please understand, we men have no problems with that. The problem arises with the fact that you women, knowing this, you have the tendency to instigate the holdup.

So while your husband is shielding you, you're behind him in the meantime, yelling, "That's right! If you want my purse, you have to *blow his head off!* [applause] And I don't think you can do it! In fact, I *dare* you to do it!"

Next thing you know, the police are at the scene of the crime: "Excuse me, ma'am. Can you explain to me what made this thief empty his Magnum into your husband's chest? I'm not quite clear on that. Why did he feel compelled to empty every chamber in his gun, reload, then do it again? I don't understand that, and I'm gathering from the expression left on your husband's face, neither did he."

As the applause rang in my ears, I said, "Thank you very much," and smiled, and took it all in. I nodded to the audience, then turned to wave at Johnny.

"Anthony Griffin!" he called out, and the camera showed him nodding and clapping. "Good job." He waved back.

He didn't motion me over to the couch, but I couldn't feel too disappointed. "Nice job. Nice job. Very nice," he was saying with a smile. "Anthony Griffin's his name. I think you'll hear more about him. We'll be right back."

The page came out to retrieve me and said, "Hey, man, you were funny. You were real funny." The band members were going, "You were funny." The tech people backstage, black and white, the people who were escorting me, and everyone whom I made contact with were saying that it was funny.

Jim McCawley shook my hand and said, "Very funny, Anthony, very funny."

Before I reached my dressing room, Buddy Morra intercepted me to say, "Very funny, kid," and patted me on the back. "You didn't look nervous."

"I was so nervous," I said.

"You couldn't tell," Buddy said. "You couldn't tell at all."

I'm a slow dresser, so I took my time getting on my clothes. I took a deep breath in and out. It was over, and nothing had gone wrong. I was thinking, *Man, now I can go home and watch it with Brigitte and Brittany.*

As I walked through the parking lot to my car, Johnny Carson was on his way to his private parking space, and we saw each other. He beckoned me over.

"Very funny, Anthony, very funny," he said. "I'm going to have you on again, so get ready to do the show a second time."

"Thank you," I said.

We shook hands.

So I was the first one to hear that I was going to return to *The Tonight Show* because I got the word from Johnny himself, not my manager, not Jim McCawley. It was a quiet, intimate conversation between the master of the show and a young comedian, and he gave me that approval. It was a special moment that I'll remember forever.

When Johnny said, "You're funny," it solidified in my mind that I *am* funny. There's always doubt when you're playing the clubs. How you fare there can depend on whether the comic who goes on in front of you is doing well or whether the audience is listening or how much people have been drinking. But doing it at such high stakes under the lights—on the most sought-after platform in all of entertainment—and to be able to say, "Hey, I was funny"— that's a big deal.

I look back and see the progression: I'm the guy who started on the West Side of Chicago, in the projects, and grew up to reach the biggest stage there is. It's like the kid playing football or baseball who gets to play in the pros. To have Johnny say "You're funny" meant I was in the private group. I was accepted.

And I would get to come back.

Johnny continued to his car, and I went to mine, drove home, gave Brigitte and Brittany big hugs, and told them all about everything. Immediately after the show aired across the country, the phone started ringing: friends from Chicago, family from Chicago, people saying, "Griff! We saw you, we saw you!"

To see a brother on *The Tonight Show* was a big thing in the community. Everybody called somebody. It was like the drumbeats of the village.

This was a good day.

10

No One Wants to Know the Jester's Pain

My humor is becoming dark, and it's biting, and it's becoming hateful, and the talent coordinator is seeing that there's a problem because NBC is all about nice.

Brigitte

I was proud of Anthony when he performed on *The Tonight Show*, but I was distracted emotionally. I was compartmentalizing everything at that point. I knew his routine, and as I watched, I was dissecting it more than enjoying it. I took note of the applause breaks and when and for how long he paused. It was very scientific for me. When it was over, I exhaled.

I hoped that everybody had tuned in to watch him. I wanted this to give a big lift to Anthony and his career. But I didn't have that "movin' on up" feeling, like on *The Jeffersons*. That wasn't part of my makeup.

Anthony was the naive and innocent one, and that served me well because he was a great balance for me. I didn't want to dash his dreams and his hopes. But I was raised in a household where the other shoe eventually was going to drop. I am a cynic at heart. I try to look at a glass as half full, but it's just not my self-talk. I prepare for the worst. I prepare to be let down. I rarely idealize situations. I know where that comes from.

I felt like we were living in a Cinderella situation. Anthony received all of these accoutrements and amenities, and sometimes he was picked up in a limousine and got to walk a red carpet. The greenrooms were great, and everybody knew him as a nice guy. Then there was the carriage-turns-to-pumpkin part, where we came home from the ball to deal with a sick child and to check her platelets, and Anthony went on the road again, and I worried about how he was being treated and whether he was standing up for himself. It took much effort to make sure that everything was okay when, in reality, it wasn't. My middle name might as well have been What if? I was always thinking about *What if?*

So I didn't make room for the joy of Anthony's triumph. He was achieving what he'd wanted, yet for me it was hard to celebrate. I turned to prayer and the Bible to find solace.

After Anthony was on *The Tonight Show*, the invitations to Hollywood parties poured in, and I was expected to go with him. From the moment I arrived, I looked for the exit. It was mostly comics and actors, but everything was a blur to me. None of it felt important. I didn't want to be bothered with this bunch of phonies. I looked at them sideways, thinking, *This person is talking to me only because of Anthony. He isn't interested in the books I'm reading or hearing about my life.* At the same time, I thought that if I was sarcastic with anyone, that might negatively affect Anthony's career, so I watered down my personality.

I understood that this was his world, so I didn't have to live in it fully. I could dip my toe in it. When Anthony was invited to parties, I had to go but preferred to be with my daughter. My joy came when I was smelling Brittany, holding her, and dressing her up. These are the moments I really, really cherished. When I was away from her, I couldn't wait to get back to her.

Anthony

Everything accelerated after I was on *The Tonight Show*. I was being introduced to important people and invited to parties, my club bookings were getting better, and I was making more money. Comics are used to putting tens of thousands of miles on their beat-up cars as they drive from gig to gig. After I moved to California, I flew more often, but it was still mostly on my dime. Now I knew I was moving up because club owners started paying a percentage of my airfare. Once I was on *The Tonight Show*, more offers included the clubs picking up my flights and putting me up in decent accommodations.

I remained optimistic about Brittany, who was in good medical hands and had been up for every challenge so far. I kept doing what I was doing.

Around this time I changed my name. I'd always been Anthony Griffin, but when I joined the Screen Actors Guild (SAG) and the American Federation of Television and Radio Artists (AFTRA), I learned that actor Tony Griffin, Merv Griffin's son, had gotten there first; his full name is Anthony Patrick Griffin. Although I found it unlikely that either of us would be confused for the other, there couldn't officially be two Anthony Griffins without his permission. He didn't grant it, so I was forced to make the change.

Three-part names were popular then (Lou Diamond Phillips, Anthony Michael Hall, Michael J. Fox, for that matter), so I suggested Anthony Van Griffin.

"No, that name's not going to work," said Buddy Morra, who didn't like the sound of that at all. Maybe I didn't look Anthony Van Griffin-ish.

I went with Anthony Griffith, though I wasn't happy about it because when I was younger, kids teased me by calling me Andy Griffith.

Brigitte didn't switch, so I'm Anthony Griffith, married to Brigitte Travis-Griffin.

When I went to the clubs at night to work on my next *Tonight Show* set, the comics were supportive and provided inspiration. Rodney Dangerfield was hot back then, and I saw him a lot because he worked at the Laugh Factory and came out in his pajamas.

The Improv also was a hub for many comics, actors, and writers. Comics booked on *The Tonight Show* came in to do guest sets, so I saw Jerry Seinfeld or George Wallace and Ellen DeGeneres—as well as Budd Friedman at his table, shaking hands with everybody. Budd had connections to get stars to his shows. After one of my performances, he introduced me to the actor James Coburn. I was a fan of his 1967 film *In Like Flint*, so that was cool, and he was a nice guy, really tall.

"Groovy, man," he told me. "You were groovy."

Budd made sure his parties were well stocked with celebrities as well. I quickly learned the etiquette: When you see someone famous, you don't point or even say, "It's great to meet you." The important thing was to act like you belonged there. Sometimes I didn't know whom I was meeting and afterward was told that so-and-so was a big-time agent or some other powerful Hollywood figure.

As a midwesterner, my only gripe was that the parties exclusively served finger food. In the black world, our thinking is, *When are we going to eat?*

Brigitte disliked Hollywood parties because when people found out she wasn't in the business, they didn't talk to her much. In general, people at these parties are always looking over your shoulder to find someone more important than you. The feeling was different from in Chicago, where when someone asks, "Do you want to get together tomorrow?" they mean, "Do you want to get together tomorrow?" In LA "Do you want to get together tomorrow?" means "Maybe we'll get together—or not."

I was so naive. While I was saying hi to everyone, Brigitte was thinking, *Yeah, this sucks.* The only thing she wanted from anyone was to make a friend, and in Hollywood that's hard.

We hadn't been living in LA that long and knew few people. There were my cousin and manager and some people from the clubs, but that was about it. I tried making friends at the comedy clubs and sought out anybody from Chicago because a lot of Chicagoans moved to LA. Still, our social circle was small.

So Brigitte, Brittany, and I were pretty much a self-contained unit. It didn't help that I still took a lot of road gigs, including, as Johnny Carson had mentioned, almost a week's worth of shows at Zanies in Chicago. As a comic, it was important to be wanted and to stay busy, but in my case that meant Brigitte spent much time home alone with Brittany.

In Chicago we had family on both sides.

In LA Brigitte felt like everything was on her shoulders.

Brigitte

When Brittany was ill, I didn't have the comfort of my family. I couldn't reach out and touch them. I loathed it. Anthony was always on the road, and I had to carry the heavy emotional weight without a support system nearby.

I didn't want to get to know anyone new because my focus was Brittany. My relationships outside the hospital were not part of my culture. I became friends with the social worker and oncology nurses and people like that. That was my village.

Anthony

We did the best we could to care for Brittany at home, but eventually we had to admit her to Children's Hospital. The high-dosage chemo was taking its toll, and the cancer wasn't going away. Even though Brittany looked like she was doing well, her platelets were low, and she needed constant care and a sterile environment.

After she was admitted to the hospital, the doctors unplugged the tracheotomy she had received in Chicago, and from then on she could communicate with us solely through sign language—as much as she could manage. The doctors kept close tabs on her heart, which had a hole in it and already had failed once.

All of the kids in her ward were bald, though by this time Brittany was used to having no hair, so to her this was normal.

There was a Ronald McDonald House near this Children's Hospital, too, but because we had an apartment in LA, we didn't need to stay there. Still, Brigitte and I spent days and many nights at the hospital, where you could sleep and shower. We took turns going home to check the mail, but for the most part we were together as a family.

My second *The Tonight Show* appearance was scheduled for October 31, 1990, Halloween. Once again I worked on my set in the clubs while Jim McCawley observed and gave me feedback. But this time the process was different and more difficult.

I kept to myself whatever was going on with Brittany. I didn't tell Jim, Buddy Morra, or anyone else in my professional circle. I was doing a lot of masking because I didn't want to make my problems anyone else's problems. I didn't want a pity party, and I didn't want to enter a room where everybody would start sniffling or saying how sorry they were. I'm already fragile. I'm already an artist, so if you're crying, I'm going to cry more. I didn't need that.

Bottom line is, I didn't feel comfortable sharing. I'm sure most people would have been totally supportive, but maybe 2 percent would have thought, *Oh, you're just trying to get attention.* That's how I looked at it, anyway. As a comic, if I see that everybody in the audience is laughing except for one guy, I focus on that person. Even if someone points out later, "But everyone else loved you!" I stay fixated on that one naysayer. I didn't want to deal with the possibility that anyone might hassle me over my daughter.

At the time I didn't think my attitude was unusual. These were the pre-Internet, pre–social media days, when not everyone knew everything about everybody. Think about how much someone like Judy Garland, who was battling her demons by self-medicating, was masking. Johnny Carson was a master masker. He had four wives, and from what it sounds like, his life wasn't always so happy, but when he came through that curtain and sat behind that desk every night, he was the man with whom you wanted to end your day. He was Johnny.

People watch comedy to get away from their own problems. They don't want to hear all about a comedian's problems.

Wait—the jester has it worse than us? This isn't fun.

So there's that fine line.

Brigitte

Would we have shared more if Facebook had been around? That's an interesting question. On social media everything is abbreviated, and people read the updates as they're multitasking. There's something organic about hearing a voice on a phone: the tone, the intonations, those rhythms. You share information and receive immediate feedback. Something about that feels right and supportive.

If all of this were going on now, we probably would share it on social media because it's part of how we communicate. But we would be cautious.

When I wanted to share information with my family, I turned to my grandmother. She was the matriarch—and our Paul Revere. She proudly accepted that role of spreading the news and was able to take some of that emotional burden from me so I didn't have to repeat the same story over and over and listen to the same responses, like, "Well, what's next?" My grandmother communicated with everyone close to us. She was our social media.

Anthony's mom was like that too. The matriarchs in the family took on that burden so it wasn't as overwhelming for Anthony and me. They were our support system. Hollywood was not.

Anthony often was on the road somewhere, so I was the one who met with the doctors as they went over Brittany's numbers and decided on the next set of treatments. When Anthony called from wherever he was performing, I gave him the update: Brittany had to undergo another round of chemo or follow a new regimen. There was always something. Things weren't getting better.

Anthony

To do your job, sometimes you must create an alternate world in your head, go into a kind of bubble. Boxers train in the mountains so they don't have to deal with whatever problems await them at home. The same is true for a comic: you block out the real world in order to go onstage and do what you do—even if what you do reflects what's going on in that world. If you can't create this separation, people will detect that something is going on. You try to clear your head for those few minutes that it's just you onstage.

Making people laugh was my talent, the skill with which I was blessed. It's what allowed me to fulfill my dream. It's my calling.

But as my sweet daughter declined, as I watched her suffer, I found that I had less and less laughter to share.

Doctors are professionals. They deal with these situations for a living. Doctors don't cry. So when our doctor came to us with tears in his eyes, we knew.

"We really can't do any more for her," he told us. "All we can offer at this point is experimental treatment."

"How long does she have?" I asked.

"Six weeks, at the most."

Six weeks. We'd planned on watching our girl grow up, to share our lives and love and so much more with her over the rest of our days. Now we had six weeks.

And my *The Tonight Show* appearance was coming up.

How do you do your job when your world is falling apart?

People ask themselves this question all the time. They face major challenges, experience horrible losses, endure unbearable traumas, yet they still must pay the bills. They still must show up for work.

How do you do your job when your world is falling apart and your job is to be *funny*?

How do you make people laugh when all you want to do is cry?

I didn't feel funny. I felt angry—at myself, at life. I did not rail at God, but I was confused, trying to figure out what was going on. Why was this happening to our beautiful girl, who might not make it to her third birthday? Why was this happening to us? What did we do? What could we have done? What could we do now, aside from watching Brittany slip from our grasp?

I looked at myself as a good guy. I didn't drink. I didn't do drugs. I went to church. I was a faithful husband and loving father. If I were drinking or getting high or cheating on my wife, I might have thought I'd somehow brought this on. But why was this happening to one of the "good guys"? And why was this happening to Brittany, who was as innocent as anyone could be? How was this fair to her or Brigitte or any of us?

Now I realize that life doesn't work like that, but at the time I was a young man who thought the world was nice, and if you believed in God, He would take care of you. I thought that as a man, I was in control. I was not.

I still had to get onstage and be funny—in front of hundreds of people in the clubs and millions of people on *The Tonight Show*. Being asked to perform for Johnny Carson twice was a blessing, yet now it felt like a curse.

So I was in far from a positive mind-set as I worked out material for my upcoming appearance. I'd been there before, so I was more confident, but I also was more torn about the material to present.

I wanted to talk about what was going on in my life, to find a way to make it funny. In the hospital, people made light of the darkest circumstances. The nurses and doctors must keep their humor up because in that environment, those who don't find some laughter amid the seriousness will be crushed. One must let in some light or spend every day crying.

But in the world beyond the hospital, people don't joke about two-year-old girls suffering from cancer and losing their hair. That's not funny.

I wasn't willing to discuss Brittany's illness in my act anyway. I couldn't reveal all that to the world.

Still, plenty of other negative thoughts stirred inside me. I reflected on being a young black man in America, all the times when I was suspected of wrongdoing solely because of the color of my skin. I thought about how police reacted to young African Americans in cars, an aggravation that didn't go away with my change in geography. Even in Hollywood I'd get pulled over: "License and registration. Is this your car? Do you live around here?"

I thought about being followed around stores, typecast as an actor, suspected of murder for no reason other than I was a tall black man standing at a bus stop. I recalled how Chicago cops pulled me over as I walked home from the hospital where my daughter lay in a coma.

Everything was building up and building up, and it had to come out somewhere. For most of my life I'd let these things go. Now I couldn't.

I'd used some of this material in my comedy before, but my tone shifted. When I arrived in Hollywood, I was goofy and bright. Over the course of Brittany's illness, I grew up quickly. Even though I wasn't talking about cancer in my sets, I was stacking one dark story atop another, presenting a bleak picture of how I was experiencing life. I thought I was the same person no matter the circumstances, but people observing me could tell something was going on even if they didn't know what.

Brigitte

Antony started getting really dark. He was still a sweet guy, but his demeanor changed. It went from fanciful and frolicsome to bitter and biting. Even his facial expressions changed when he would deliver his bits. He came across as angry.

He didn't try out his routines at home per se. His way was more circuitous. He practiced on me in conversation, making various grim observations without ever asking "Honey, what do you think of this?" While talking things through with me, he got a feel for whether something was funny. If it was, the next thing I knew, it showed up onstage.

I laughed at the dark stuff. I really did. He told me later that's when he knew he could try this material onstage, after getting my initial response.

Anthony

Jim McCawley noticed the change. I told some jokes, and he asked, "Do you really want to do that?"

"Yes, I really do."

I got onstage and performed sets that reflected my mood. I had one bit about shopping for a Honda Accord:

> I was somewhat scared to buy the car at first, to tell you the truth, because of the salesman. The salesman would say things like, "Check out the trunk space [pause]. You notice how big that is? [pause] Now let's say for instance that you were to [long pause, shakes head] . . . oh, I don't know, uh [pause] . . . shoot your wife in the face. Just as an example. Now with the Honda, you can place your wife's body and the sawed-off shotgun in the trunk–yet still have room enough for your golf clubs.
>
> And I rush home: "Honey, I got a car, a Honda Accord!"
>
> [Yelling as wife] "Honda! Now what the hell you get a Honda for? Of all the cars you could've got, what's so damned special about the Honda?"
>
> "Trunk space."
>
> "I don't get it."
>
> "You will. Don't worry about it."

Brigitte

I love that bit.

Anthony

Afterward, Jim said, "What else have you got?" That meant no. It meant "This is not for *The Tonight Show*." It meant "Is there anything that would lighten up this set?"

Jim didn't confront me directly; he was subtler than that. He did have a conversation with my manager, though, and Buddy passed along the message to me: "Just have a lighter tone."

Again, they had no idea what was going on in my life. All they were looking at was what audiences expected to entertain them late at night on NBC.

Brigitte

Anthony started coming home from the clubs complaining that Jim and the others felt his stuff was too biting, too angry, too gritty. They wanted him to keep it Midwest light.

Anthony

Even Richard Pryor kept it light on *The Tonight Show*. I needed to be the clown who amused the audience like I did the first time they saw me. The message I was getting from Jim was that I had to be funny, funny, funny, but I wasn't feeling even *one* funny, never mind three. I wasn't that goofy guy anymore.

Times have changed since then, and darker humor is more widely accepted. If I did that Honda bit now, no one would give it a second thought.

But in 1990, *The Tonight Show* dominated late-night comedy, my humor had grown out of sync, and Jim McCawley and I were butting heads.

11

The Second 'Tonight' Set

I hate dogs. People say a dog's a man's best friend. I have
yet to have a best friend poop in my living room.

Anthony

It was Halloween 1990, the day of my second *Tonight Show* appearance, and
Brigitte, Brittany, and I were together in the hospital. I put a little tape around
Brittany's hands and on the base of her nose to make her look like a boxer
about to work out. That humor went over in the hospital, though I'm not sure
how it would have played on the outside.

I thought of doing my own Halloween dress-up for *The Tonight Show* as
well. I had the hilarious idea of coming out in a dress and not mentioning it
at any point during my appearance. I actually brought the dress to the studio,
and when Buddy saw it in my dressing room, he said, "What are you doing?"

"I thought it would be funny," I said.

"Oh, man," he said. "Don't."

I didn't. Good thing too. Actor/comedian Kevin Pollak was on the same
show and came out dressed as Cupid. Johnny didn't look particularly amused.

Brigitte once again wasn't with me at the studio, choosing, with good
reason, to stay at the hospital with Brittany. I was on my own, but this time
without the jitters I felt before my first appearance. Now I had more experience,

as well as a deeper, broader perspective on life. Appearing on *The Tonight Show* no longer was my most pressing issue.

After the difficult back-and-forth with Jim McCawley, we settled on a set that channeled some of my anger in a not-too-confrontational way while also including more innocuous material.

As I stood behind the curtain for the second time, I heard Johnny's introduction:

> He's a regular at the Improv in Hollywood; he's going to be at a new club in San Ramon, California, the twelfth of December, called Tommy T's; and you may have seen him on Ed's show *Star Search*, where he was a finalist.
>
> ["Yes," Ed McMahon chimed in.]
>
> Would you welcome Anthony Griffith. Anthony!

I wore a maroon shirt and dark slacks and looked comfortable and relaxed. I began by putting a spin on my racially profiled past:

> I just moved here to California from Chicago [cheers]. Came out here to pursue my acting career. I first started performing in college. I majored in theater, but my school would only put on plays like *Oklahoma!* and *Annie Get Your Gun*—plays in which I really couldn't showcase all my talents. I just got tired of saying things like, "Mo' biscuits, sir?"
>
> I was a butler in just about every play while I was in college. In fact, I was a butler in plays that didn't have butlers. Believe it or not, I was a butler in *West Side Story*. People would come up to me: "Do you know where Maria is?"
>
> "I don't know where Maria is. I know where the biscuits are."
>
> And at the time that I left Chicago, every twelve seconds a crime was being committed in the city, which was scary—especially to me because that meant every twelve seconds I was a suspect. It used to amaze me how I could walk into the store, and every eye would watch me simply because I tan easier than most people. Whenever I touched something . . .

"May I help you?"

"No, I'm just looking."

"What are you looking for?"

"I'm just looking."

"What *exactly* are you looking for?"

"Well, right now I'm looking for a can of Raid to make you stop bugging me" [applause, whistles].

Then I delivered a fanciful variation on my errant murder arrest:

In fact, I was mistakenly arrested for attempted murder once. It was funny to me how it happened because I was working out at a health spa, and I was in the process of taking off my gym shoes and socks, and the police came up to me and said, "You're under arrest for attempted murder."

And I just started laughing. I just went, "Wait a minute, Officer. Now, I know my socks stink, but they don't smell that bad."

I mean, that's what I thought because my father used to always tell me, "One of these days your gym socks are going to kill somebody."

And they took me to the hospital to be identified by the victim, which was frightening, until I saw the victim was delirious. He just looked up at me and started saying, "Mama? Mama, is that you?"

And I played right along. I said, "Yeah, it's me, baby."

I wasn't going to jail, man. Not as skinny as I am. It's nice to be loved, but . . .

[looked around; applause]

The rest of the set was more of my standard stuff, as I riffed on widely relatable issues. For instance, expensive gym shoes:

Kids literally beg their parents for Air Jordans. You'll see them in stores everywhere you go:

"Mama, I've gotta have the Air Jordans! I gotta be like Michael!"

"Well, until you bring home three million dollars like Michael, I'm taking your butt to Payless" [applause].

Gym shoes are so mainstream in our society. I read an article where a shoe company sent five hundred boxes of gym shoes to Ethiopia in hopes of reducing the famine. As if the Ethiopians would look at these boxes and go, "You know, Desmond, now that we have these gym shoes, I think we can catch that cheetah going seventy-five miles an hour" [applause].

I can just picture Ethiopians behind a bush going, "Here, cheetah cheetah cheetah cheetah. Man, there he go, right over there! Oh man, no wonder we can't catch him. He wearing gym shoes too!" [applause]

I expanded on my bit about dogs from *Star Search*, including the part about my dog calling me from a pay phone after a fire, and this:

And in Chicago if your dog poops in public, by law you're supposed to pick up the poop. Now, after, say, a week of doing this, you've got to ask yourself: *Who's the real master in this relationship?*

Then you have people who dress their dogs. One of the most embarrassing moments in my life happened one time on my way to work. A dog crossed my path wearing a sweater and a matching cap. And I just so happened to be wearing that same outfit.

I received seven applause breaks, and they were strong, though I wasn't counting at the time. Doc's band kicked in, and I thanked and waved to the audience. I turned toward Johnny with one finger in the air and waved to him as well. He was smiling and applauding, though again he didn't call me over to his desk. At that point, whether or not I received the coveted desk invitation didn't even register with me.

"Anthony Griffith! Thank you, Anthony!" he said, clapping and then looking at the camera. "We'll be back." He turned back toward me and clapped again. "Good job! Nice job!"

I didn't linger afterward. I left the NBC lot and rushed back to the hospital, where Brigitte, Brittany, and I watched the show's broadcast. Despite the circumstances, I was able to laugh. It was a strong set, and the three of us were together.

We didn't enjoy this triumph for long.

12

The Final Days

I had a baby girl not too long ago . . .

Brigitte

Early in Brittany's life, my biggest fear was that Anthony or I would leave this earth, and she would have no one to take care of her. That's what I worried about as a parent because she couldn't take care of herself.

But God forbid something would happen to her.

Life in the hospital was so grim, so sobering. Anthony was on the road a lot, and I was there all the time. Some days she would be so sick that I would say to God, "Just let her fall asleep and not wake up. This would be ideal. This is a best-case scenario. Just let me call in that chip right quick."

Brittany made friends with kids and had roommates who were gone a week later. They succumbed to their disease. I saw a *lot* of death.

There was one boy, Michael, who was very verbal. With her tracheotomy and the fact that she was nonverbal, there was so much that Brittany could not communicate. Seeing this, Michael tried to help out by telling us what he thought she was going through. One time Brittany had a bad reaction to some meds and entered a delirious state with nightmarish hallucinations. It was terrifying, but Michael told us what being in such a state felt like, which helped. He was a sweet kid. I think his grandmother showed up once, but otherwise he didn't have visitors.

One of the worst parts about arriving at Children's Hospital's oncology unit was that when you got off the elevator, you never knew whose room might all of a sudden be empty. One day it was Michael's room. He was gone.

Brittany had one roommate whose mother was dealing with her own issues and her own denial because her daughter was gravely ill. She was the sweetest little preschooler, and her mother kept asking her to perform.

"Show 'em, honey! Sing! Dance!"

You could see from the look on this brave child's face that she wanted permission to just float away, float away and be separate from her body. This sweet little warrior seemed like she stayed on this earth longer than she desired just to appease her mom—because her mom was putting all she could into keeping her alive. That one broke my heart.

One day I arrived to find the grandmother standing outside her room. Sometimes there are no words. The grandmother shook her head, and I gave her a hug. On the Children's Hospital's pediatric oncology floor, it was like all of the adults—no matter our native country or language or dialect or garb—collectively knew when another sweet angel had earned his or her heavenly wings, and we shared a moment of silence.

The grandmother finally said to me in an exhausted whisper, "I thought Brittany was going to be first."

I understood. She was in her grief, a very new grief.

Also on the floor was a junior pastor from a megachurch in the San Fernando Valley. A prayer team came out every day and huddled in the corner of an isolated nearby stairway. I thought, *Wow, he has his parishioners here—his family, his church family.* Anthony and I had to get on the phone and ask for prayer over the speakerphone. This was powerful.

Brittany survived him too. Although she shared the company of at least a dozen roommates, many of whom became her playmates, four or five of her friends made their final transition before her.

Every time I got off the elevator on her floor, my stomach knotted up in fear of what awaited me. I hardly ate because I was afraid to go down to the cafeteria; God only knew what I'd discover upon my return. I was on pins and needles all the time, always at the ready.

One day, when I'd been in Brittany's room for many hours, a nurse told me, "Take a soak bath, Bridge. Take a soak bath just to relax."

So I went down the hall and treated myself to a nice, long bath. I needed that. I convinced myself that I deserved that.

But when I came back, Brittany's room was empty.

Oh, Lord Jesus. I almost tore that place apart.

It turned out the nurses had moved Brittany to another room. The head nurse was very apologetic.

"We will never do that again," she told me. "That was not okay. You don't do that. We just wanted you to relax."

I never took a soak bath again. Not there, at least.

Anthony

Brittany still loved to eat; the tracheotomy didn't affect that, though sometimes her treatments made her lose her appetite. She was still our little girl, and it was hard to see her suffering.

We spent a lot of time dealing with complications from her treatment. With the chemotherapy pumping so many toxins into her system, Brittany's body would get swollen, and the medical team worked to keep her fluid levels down. Throughout all of their work, the nurses remained steady and resilient. They couldn't break down in front of the parents. Maybe they did so in private, but with us they kept it together.

I know exactly when Brittany was born, how long her delivery was. It was thirty-three minutes. She was born at 4:33 a.m. But I do not remember her death. My mind blocks it out. I know it was November something, 20 or 22, 1990.

I'd slept at the hospital the night before, and in the morning I went back to the house to take a shower and pick up the mail. I leaned down and gave Brittany a kiss, and she looked up at me with her sweet eyes. I remember that she looked up at me.

Brigitte

Brittany had an infection that was eroding one of her arteries. She was not going to survive this. We knew. She eventually would succumb to the infection, get a high fever, probably go into cardiac arrest.

The doctors understood that I was someone who needed to know everything, and they were very good at keeping me informed. But I think Brittany's main doctor withheld some information from me intentionally, which was a good thing because I didn't know the worst-case scenario.

Tony had gone home to take a shower, and the respiratory therapist came in to do her work. All of a sudden, the therapist jumped—because she saw the blood. Something had caused Brittany to hemorrhage.

I ran to the nurse's station.

"We need someone *right now*," I said.

After returning with the medical team, I'll never forget the look on my daughter's face. She was looking up at all of these adults standing around her with an expression of panic, like a child drowning.

My prayer was that she would lose consciousness immediately. It felt like it went on for hours, but it was actually something like forty-five seconds. She hemorrhaged to death.

Right afterward, her social worker told me, "We need to get you out of these clothes."

I didn't realize my clothes were covered with blood. From that day on, I could never eat red meat because of the smell of the blood. It's an olfactory association that I have never shaken.

Years later I learned that I had PTSD from this experience. Yet I also knew this: I was there, and I had honored my daughter. It's an honor to be there when a child is born, and I considered it an honor to hold my child as she transitioned to a place of holy healing.

Anthony

After showering and taking care of some quick business at home, I made two stops on the way back to the hospital: I picked up some fresh flowers and then some food from my favorite fish place. At the hospital the social worker was waiting for me by the elevator on Brittany's floor with an urgent look in her eyes. When we reached the room, Brittany was in Brigitte's arms. She had passed.

The nurses had cleaned her up to make her presentable and had removed all the equipment that had been attached to her. She didn't need any of that anymore.

She looked like a girl sleeping in her mother's arms. She looked like the daughter she had been so many months earlier in her bed or crib, before she needed to be hooked up to so much technology. She was still warm to the touch. I was hurting, but I didn't want my child to be in pain anymore. I didn't want her to go through any more anguish. No longer was anything in disarray. She was at peace.

Brigitte had been crying, of course, but she was strong. As I've always said, she's the strongest one. I don't remember saying anything. It was a peaceful, quiet moment. We sat there together for a long time, the three of us, and eventually my wife and I fell asleep.

13

The Aftermath

I wake up saying, "I'm sorry":
"Good morning, honey."
"I'm sorry."
"What are you sorry for?"
"I don't know yet. I'm just trying to earn some extra credit."

Brigitte

About a week after Brittany lost her battle with leukemia, Anthony was back on the road, and I entered the darkest period of my life.

Before that, we'd had a service for Brittany in LA, and then we all flew back to Chicago for her homegoing service at Merrill Avenue Baptist Church, where Anthony and I had gotten married just a few years earlier. Brittany was buried in Washington Memorial Cemetery in the south suburbs, and the funeral director had a wonderful surprise awaiting us. The plot we had selected for her was deep into the cemetery, but as we found out on the day of her burial, they had decided to place her by the children's pond instead. It's a beautiful pond, near the cemetery's entrance, with ducks all around.

"They don't usually do that," my aunt said.

It was a lovely gesture.

Unfortunately, I couldn't escape this funeral experience without some drama from my mother. Before we left for Chicago, my mother left a message: "This is your mother. Give me a call."

The sound of her voice made me shudder. I had not spoken with her since Brittany, Anthony, and I had relocated to Los Angeles. The message carried her usual intonation of impending verbal abuse. I had neither the emotional energy nor the desperate hopefulness to return the call.

Then, before the burial service, the funeral director informed me, "Your mom doesn't want to sign the guest book with anyone else's name on it but hers."

"Well, I don't know how that's going to work," I said.

"Don't worry about it," he said. "We'll have a separate book for her just so she can have her name in it." This funeral director must have been well versed in averting family conflicts.

My aunt tried to get me to talk with her, but I said, "Absolutely not. You guys didn't advocate for me then. Now I'm advocating for myself."

A pastor later counseled me about my guilt associated with my mother's lack of emotional attachment and my resulting emotional distance. "We're supposed to protect children," he told me. "You were not protected. Now you are in self-protection mode, and this is how you take care of yourself. It's okay. That is not a sin. What's important is that you respect your caregivers."

Soon we were back home in Los Angeles, away from all of my family again. My role had changed, as well as my title. I was no longer to be identified as the mom of Brittany Nicole Griffin, but I was still the wife of Anthony Griffin—or now, as everyone knew him, Anthony Griffith. I wasn't identifying myself as an individual. I had no voice of my own and, I thought, no one to stand up for me.

I entered a period of chronic heartache—overwhelmed with loneliness, despair, and never-ending ruminations on how I might have done things differently, how I might have changed the trajectory of Brittany's life span. I replayed so many different narratives in my head, which impaired my ability to sleep. I even shamed myself for wanting to fall into slumber.

At first, when I slept, I experienced lucid dreams that allowed me some control over a situation. Most of my dreams were about Brittany, which I welcomed; I yearned for that heavenly escape each night. But as my sleep grew more disturbed, my pleasant dreams became less frequent, and recurrent nightmares took hold. To avoid the nightmares, I fought sleep even more, and my thinking and perceptions of reality grew increasingly distorted.

I perceived that Anthony wasn't skipping a beat. He was getting on with his life, hitting the road, paying the bills, and he didn't stop to consider what was happening with me. I was angry with him. I was angry for feeling abandoned. He became less of a sounding board, as a large part of me perceived that he lacked the fortitude to support me through my grief, that he wasn't emotionally strong enough. I allowed myself to believe that if he didn't have the skills to stand up for himself against the club-owner bullies, there was no way he could support me or even conceptualize how much I missed Brittany.

I was home alone and despairing. I experienced persistent pessimistic thoughts that my world would never be bright again. I wanted to escape the loneliness, and I started to consider my options. I rationalized that it made more sense for me to be with Brittany on the other side than isolated in a town with no familial support. Reuniting with Brittany became my paramount thought over those days and weeks. I longed for that. She had been my entire life. All I wanted was to have her back.

But I dared not say the *S*-word aloud—couldn't even think it. I attempted all manner of cognitive calisthenics to reframe what I was contemplating.

I tried to devise ways I could end my earthly existence and still go to heaven so I could be with Brittany. My thoughts included fleeting plans about consuming a narcotic cocktail, though thankfully I didn't have the means to obtain any lethal polysubstances. I never contemplated asphyxiation or slitting my wrists, jumping from a dangerously high structure, or using a firearm. We women don't turn guns on ourselves. Besides, I remember thinking, *Why would I further traumatize a stranger or loved one who might have the misfortune of finding me in that state?*

I went through a laundry list of "what-if" scenarios. As a bereft young parent, I didn't realize at that time that such thoughts were irrational—if also not unusual for someone enduring such circumstances.

Whatever I did, I didn't want to look ugly doing it. For one, I wanted my eyebrows done—because God forbid I ended up in a coma, I couldn't trust Anthony to make sure my brows were done and my toenails were polished and stuff like that. He would say, "Oh, her eyebrows are fine," even if they were bushy. I tell my friends and Tony now, "If anything happens to me, and I can't lift my arms and blink, you all have to come in and make sure to pluck my eyebrows and do my toenails."

I kept trying to think of ways to take my own life so I could see my daughter again.

But if I killed myself, would I wind up in purgatory? Or would I go to hell? I was raised Catholic and Muslim, so these questions were all the more confusing.

Getting through each day was rough. So many things triggered me: music, smells, hearing babies cry or coo. Just seeing a child sometimes put me into a tailspin.

Ending my life was such a temptation dangling there. I constantly had to pray, read the Word, and talk myself out of it. If my goal was to see my daughter as soon as possible, then I didn't want to circumvent that process and unknowingly screw it up. I was determined to make my next meeting with Brittany as Jesus-endorsed as possible, so I engrossed myself in increasingly benevolent activities while opening the door to the Holy Spirit. The contract is void if you kill yourself, and I needed to be in heaven with my girl.

I still do, so here I am.

Anthony

I was shocked that Brigitte ever contemplated suicide. I didn't find out until years later that she considered taking such an extreme step to be with Brittany again. That's something I never would have thought about.

Brigitte loved being a mom. She loved having her daughter in her lap and just chilling out, the two of them. Motherhood was an essential part of her and her identity. I enjoyed being a father but never had that intense level of connection and identification.

It was eye-opening to me that she felt so sad and alone that she weighed taking her own life. We grieved as a couple, but Brigitte's own grief was even deeper than what we experienced together. I wouldn't say I had less grief, but it was just different. Brigitte and I talked about this, and she felt I wasn't grieving as much. I had to tell her, "Men and women—and individuals—grieve differently." Even now sometimes I feel like I must remind her: "Hey,

I'm not you. I'm different from you. I'm a dude, for one. I'm not one of your girlfriends."

I keep things to myself. I was able to grieve more openly when I was around my mom because then I could be the little boy again. With Brigitte I was the husband, and I didn't let down my guard so much.

Instead, I kept everything bottled up, and sometimes it came out in weird ways. For a long time after Brittany passed, I couldn't park the car correctly. I could not do that to save my life. I would get frustrated: *How come I can't park the car?* I don't know if people knew I was hurting. I just knew that all of a sudden I could not park a car or do even simple things. I think that was the grief expressing itself.

Beyond a close circle of friends and family, no one knew what Brigitte and I had been through. Now when an entertainer, even someone as early in his career as I was, loses a child, someone from TMZ points a phone camera at him and asks, "How are you doing?" This was the kind of story that also would play on *Access Hollywood* (which wasn't around yet) and *Entertainment Tonight* (which was).

Yet everything with Brigitte and me was quiet. We received support from some friends in the industry, such as future *Freaks and Geeks* creator Paul Feig, whom I met while we were both doing stand-up, and his soon-to-be wife, Laurie Karon. But I hadn't even told Buddy Morra, my manager.

I was a member of the same church that is my spiritual home today: Calvary Baptist Church in Pacoima. I was there constantly and stayed involved, yet I wasn't close enough to any congregants to tell them about my loss or spiritual struggles. I don't think the pastor even knew—or if he did, he never said anything. He did not address me unless I addressed him, even though I was an active participant in the church. And I was not sharing the details of my life, even with him.

I often wondered what I would ask God when I got to the other side. My big question was a simple one: Why? Why did Brittany have to pass when I'm a believer?

Yet I was fearful to ask that in case the answer was something I had done. That would have rocked me.

If I could go back in time and tell a young Anthony anything, it would be, "There will be times when you'll be angry or sad, and it's okay to feel everything that you're feeling right now. There's nothing wrong or bad about it. You're in mourning."

I'd also say, "Going into therapy might help."

At the time therapy didn't occur to me. For blacks, that's not what we did. I didn't know anybody who had ever done it. No one asked me whether I'd consider it. No one discussed it.

Why was therapy such a taboo in the black community? Because in the black world that means you're broken; something's wrong with you. That attitude has been passed on and on.

But in essence you *are* broken. You've had trauma. African Americans as a whole have had trauma ever since slavery, and we have yet to have therapy concerning our difficult history. We have never acknowledged that we are in pain and need help.

Everyone needs a sounding board or someone to understand them. Church is a big help, but even the pastors looked at therapy as suspect. The common attitude in the community was you don't need therapy, you just need Jesus, you just need God. Many folks would say, "All you need to do is go to church." We didn't think, *Well, maybe God placed therapists among us to help us.*

As Brigitte likes to say, you have to take care of yourself. If that means therapy, taking time out, getting away from everyone, then do it.

We also have this attitude of *There's nothing wrong with me.* We think we can't show weakness. We're afraid we'll be labeled as crazy.

In the black community, we always knew who was crazy, who was "touched," and who was a little off. These were three different levels:

"He's touched. He's not going to hurt anybody because he's touched."

"He's off. You've got to excuse him because he off."

"He's crazy. He could hurt you."

Now if I were speaking with someone who had endured the kind of trauma that I had, I would ask, "What is your walk when it comes to God?" If that person didn't believe in God, I would definitely suggest therapy. If that person did believe in God, I would suggest exploring Scripture as well as therapy. These two things can go together.

I did not have therapy at the time, and I wasn't digging into Scripture either. My big thing was I really have to trust you to share anything personal with you. Even when I finally went to therapy years later, I didn't mention Brittany until one of the last sessions.

"Why didn't you tell me this two weeks ago?" the therapist asked.

I didn't trust even him. Maybe I should go into therapy to explore why I don't trust people.

It probably started when my biological father would say he was coming to pick us up but never did. That's when I learned you can't always take people at their word. Then I got to Hollywood, where words and actions rarely go together. If I say I'm going to do something, I do it.

Brigitte, who starts off from a position of not trusting, says I'm a more optimistic person, but if you hurt me once, you'll never get that trust back. I will smile to your face but put a mark next to your name. So maybe the issue isn't that I don't trust people so much as I'm a naturally trusting person who gets let down by individuals and their frailties. That's how I look at it. We all have shortcomings.

I was in pain but didn't know I was in pain, and I thought that working would get me through my grief. I didn't take time off. I worked to keep busy, and that was really hard on Brigitte because she was by herself in California without her daughter and her husband.

We had mounting bills, including expenses from Brittany's care, so I kept busy doing stand-up on the road and auditioning for TV shows and movies closer to home. I'd been on *The Tonight Show* twice, and the opportunities were pouring in, including an invitation to perform for Johnny Carson a third time.

To the outside world, I was on an upward trajectory. I tried to act that way too. But if you paid attention to the content of my act, you could perceive some key differences. What I talked about onstage had always been based on my life, yet how could I discuss my life now, when I was in so much pain and keeping so much hidden?

I was on autopilot.

Brigitte

We grieved differently and separately. I think it may be a function of culture and gender. The male tribe naturally has things in common, but at the same time there are nuances to how a black male grieves compared to a white male. Females obviously grieve differently from males, and black females, well, that's another story.

Tony's grieving process and mine were both internal. We minimized our feelings. He used a lot of distractions because he needed to. When I allowed myself to be distracted, I became racked with guilt. No, I couldn't feel happy. I couldn't smile.

I can see how grieving couples either fall apart or grow apart until they have nothing in common but that child who died.

14

The Third 'Tonight' Set

I enjoy performing. I started out in college. I did other
things in college. I played basketball, very little. I used to
say I was known as a minute man.
"Coach, can I play now?"
"In a minute, man."

Anthony

On March 20, 1991, I appeared on *The Tonight Show Starring Johnny Carson*
for the third time in just over eight months. I had a completely different mind-
set for each one.

The first time I was nervous, daunted by the prospect of standing under
those hot lights with cameras in my face while I tried to make eighteen million
people laugh without embarrassing myself. The second time I knew where to
stand, what to expect, and how to handle myself, but my preparations had
been fraught with tension—externally in my creative conflicts with talent
coordinator Jim McCawley, and internally in my struggles to tap into my
dwindling source of humor while our daughter's health was plummeting.

Now that Brittany was gone, nothing seemed so important to me anymore.
The Tonight Show was just a TV show, no big deal. My life with Brittany and
Brigitte was what had been real. I felt the freedom of "I don't care"—because I

didn't care as much about being on *The Tonight Show* or what people thought of me.

So I was relatively relaxed and confident as I approached the show. I was becoming a regular. I'd joined the club.

Although Jim McCawley still consulted with me as I assembled my set, he wasn't as much of a presence. He was still there because that was his job, but I had a longer leash. By now he trusted me, and I knew what he wanted, so he didn't have to ask, "What else have you got?" I had some material I thought would work, and he agreed with an "Okay, good."

This was the lightest of my three *Tonight Show* sets. There was nothing deeply personal here. The jokes were *jokes*, many of which I'd used previously, including on *Star Search*. I even hauled out an impression, something I hadn't been doing much in recent sets.

You could say doing an impression—of Jimmy Stewart, in this case—was a throwback for me. I don't remember why I didn't present this bit to Jim McCawley before my first appearance on the show. Maybe I thought it wasn't my strongest material. Or maybe I had just decided to have fun, something I couldn't do in either of my first two appearances.

It was like going to the Comedy & Magic Club and feeling like one of the guys: *Yeah, this is my room; I'm going to do what I feel like doing.* I could take the chance to do the Jimmy Stewart gag because it was funny and would be accepted. I wouldn't have had the courage to try it my first time.

I bought a navy blue silk suit for the show. It cost $700. Before then I could not fathom paying $700 for a suit. I would pay $99 for a suit, and that included a tie and shirt. I couldn't really see the difference between the $99 suit and the $700 suit, but Brigitte could, my agent could, and anyone who understood style or what it looked like to get to the next level could. You had to look the part as well as have the goods. Anyway, the suit was very nice, and I felt good in it.

Brigitte

After staying with Brittany during Anthony's first two *Tonight Show* appearances, I was finally able to go to the third one but got lost on the way to NBC Studios and wasn't happy about it. I was taking Brittany's social worker, Evelyn, with whom I'd grown close. She's one of the people who kept in touch with me after Brittany passed away. I'd become friends with some of the nurses as well.

Evelyn and I were driving around Burbank, looking for NBC Studios, and we went through a notoriously weird intersection that turned me around. I'd wanted to arrive early to get settled in and to check in with Anthony. Now I was worried that we would miss the taping. Once we found the studio, we still would have to go through the protocol of having our names on the list and being waved onto the lot.

Evelyn was being very casual. "Oh, if we miss it, we can see it on television tonight," she said.

Wow. This was a big deal for me and for Anthony. She was making a casual comment to try to make me feel better, but I was irritated with her. I needed to be there to support my husband.

I pulled over to ask someone where to find NBC Studios. After driving around some more, we finally made it.

Time seemed to stand still as we got onto the lot and into the building. People with headphones led us back to Anthony's dressing room. I could see from the look on his face that he needed to be alone. Getting into a private, quiet space is a must for him before he goes onstage.

Evelyn went out to be seated in the audience, but I stayed back in the greenroom. I wanted Evelyn to be able to respond naturally to the show without waiting for my cue to laugh. Plus, I couldn't handle being in the audience. I didn't want company. I preferred to be by myself.

I knew his set. I knew it almost better than Anthony did. I knew the beats. I knew the importance of waiting for a laugh break. I knew the technical side of it. I knew that it was very, very important for him to pause—but not for too long because he didn't want the audience to think he'd lost his place. I literally would hold my breath during the dramatic pauses before he delivered the next punch line.

I sat down in front of the monitor and watched.

Anthony

The other guests that night were John Larroquette, who was starring in the popular sitcom *Night Court*, and humor writer Roy Blount Jr., who later that year would release a book called *Camels Are Easy, Comedy's Hard*. No kidding. I didn't see them backstage. I don't remember ever interacting with any of the stars who were on *The Tonight Show* the same night I was.

As I stood backstage, I heard that oh-so-familiar voice saying, "Anthony Griffith has been with us before . . . ," and then promoting more of my upcoming gigs in the Chicago area, where I returned a lot because it still was my home, and audiences and club owners there knew me and saw me as a local success story.

Meanwhile, I was feeling more at home right where I was: behind *The Tonight Show* curtain.

"Will you welcome Anthony Griffith. Anthony!"

I stepped out confidently in my fancy suit.

I didn't know how to grieve. I didn't know how to process my immense pain. I didn't know how to play the role of a father who no longer had a child. I didn't know how to be there fully for my wife who was suffering. But I knew how to make people laugh. I knew how to do what I was about to do.

I had this.

Thank you very much. Glad to be back here in California. I just came back from Chicago, my birthplace. I hadn't planned on going to Chicago. I had an offer to perform on a cruise ship, which I immediately declined, of course. I don't know everything about my African culture, but I know enough to assure you the last thing I want to do in life is go on a long boat ride.

[Ed McMahon laughs loudly in the background.]

I think the last brother that did that had to change his name to Toby.

That was about as pointed as the set got. From there I went backward, to the days before I'd met my wife and started a family:

But while I was in Chicago, I was able to participate in a seminar to develop ways to fight drug abuse for our youngsters. And one way I came up with was to simply show them pictures of what we used to wear in the '60s and '70s: "You see this shirt with the collar going all the way down to the elbow? This is what happens when you take drugs" [applause].

We looked real silly back then, didn't we? I know I did. I had an Afro that was this big [gestures] in the '70s. It weighed more than my whole body.

I continued on the nostalgia trip with an extended riff that played off my mom's having been cross-eyed.

I never knew what cross-eyed meant at the age of five. All I knew was that whenever Momma would yell, "Come here!" I'd look up, see she wasn't looking directly at me, so I would just go about my business.

And she would confuse the whole family, not just me. Once we were all in a department store, and she said, "Come here, boy."

And I looked up, and I saw one eye focused over my head and the other eye going to the left, so I turned to my brother and said, "Danny, Momma's calling you."

But from Danny's perspective, one eye was going over his head, and the other eye was going to the right, so he said, "Uh-uh, she calling you."

Even the security guard at the store looked at my mother and went, "Are you talking to me, ma'am?"

And she started shouting at me, "How come you ain't come when I call?"

"Momma, I didn't know who you were talking to."

"Who you think I was talking to, that girl over there?"

Now, I'm really lost because she's looking left, she's pointing right, and there's not a girl in the store. And I'm begging her, "What girl, Momma?"

"The girl over there!"

"What girl?"

"The girl over there in that store across the street behind that pole on the second floor, sitting down brushing her hair! [applause] Now if you got something wrong with your eyes, boy, you let me know, and I'll take you to a proctologist" [big laughs, applause].

"Why a proctologist?"

"So I can get my foot out your behind from causing me so much aggravation" [more laughs and applause].

Then came the Jimmy Stewart impression:

"Why . . . why . . . why, Burt. Nick, Ernie, it's me. Don't you recognize me? It's George. George Bailey! I'm alive! Burt, Burt, remember when Potter tried to buy you out? You came to Bailey Savings and Loan for help" [applause].

That was my version of *It's a Wonderful Life* . . . colorized [applause].

Colorization of movies was a new thing at that time, but that joke still was steeped in the past, as was the quick riff that followed on my college-basketball-playing days. I closed with the Mike Tyson routine that had been a staple of my act since before I performed it on *Star Search*. I landed the key laugh lines:

. . . nothing more than a pit bull that's been trained to walk on his hind legs and fight.

He literally hit this man so hard, the blood splattered on my face. And I was watching the fight in my living room.

"Hey, you know, I'm coming back. I'm gonna just take the next year and a half to basically concentrate on, uh, breathing [applause]. Hopefully, with the help of my trainer, we can pursue other matters, such as finding out who am I and which evil spirit possessed me to get into the ring with that man" [applause].

Since I was on *Star Search*, I'd added this:

And people always say Mike Tyson is stupid. Mike Tyson made over twenty-eight million dollars last year. If that's stupid, I pray to God

I'm stupid one day. In fact, I don't want to be that rich. If I could make it to mentally unstable, I'll be set for the rest of my life.

I ended my set with the part about how I'd rather fight my mom than Tyson.

I tried to hit my mother one time, and she looked at me and said, "If you ever hit me, that'll be the last thing you ever do." And I knew she was dead serious just by the way she cocked that gun to my head.

Thank you very much.

The applause rang out. I hadn't broken any new ground. I hadn't revealed anything deep about myself. I was a professional who had done my job.

But I'd done it well. People laughed, and once again I earned numerous applause breaks. Johnny, as always, looked pleased as he clapped from his seat. I nodded his way. I still didn't get the invitation to the couch, but by then I wasn't so invested in that either. The two of us never had another conversation after our private chat in the parking lot after my first *Tonight Show* appearance, but the man was laughing at me, applauding for me, confirming to the world—and to me—that I was funny.

"Anthony Griffith!" he announced. "We'll be back in a moment."

15

The Zombie March

I appreciate the laughter because I was booed offstage
last week. At a benefit. So I was booed offstage for free.

Anthony

That was my last *Tonight Show* appearance until Jay Leno took over. When
Brigitte and I got home, I had a feeling of letdown. I'd spent all my energy
getting onto *The Tonight Show*, and I'd done it three times. I was like a boxer
who'd finally beaten the champ and then thought, *Now what?* I'd made it,
but given all that had happened in my life in the meantime, nothing felt like
it truly mattered.

Brigitte

We were like walking zombies. I was just going through the motions. I was in
a fetal position emotionally for at least nine years.

Anthony

Ten years. You do things by rote. You're depressed. You don't hear the birds
chirping. You don't smell the roses. But you go about life.

For those ten years, we did not really celebrate holidays. We were just going through the motions. You do this, you do that, but there was really no joy.

We both were rail thin.

Brigitte

There's a picture of me at a friend's house, which was taken right after Brittany passed away, and I was skeletal. I was just sitting there in a chair. Years later I would reflect back and think, *Wow! I can't remember having fun, going out on a date, having an awesome time as an adult*, because I was in this holding pattern.

When people said, "Smile," I smiled. But they didn't know. They really, really didn't know.

What I couldn't tolerate was complaining. After Brittany passed away, I would see parents being so impatient with their children—moms with their toddlers or babies. You have a child who can crawl or walk? You have a toddler who can toddle? And you're seeing it as a problem that you can't always keep up with that baby? Your child is learning to explore his or her world, and you're seeing that as a negative?

I didn't see any of those things as negatives with Brittany. I knew we had a limited time together. I'd hear parents complain, "Oh, I have to childproof everything!" I didn't have the opportunity to childproof everything.

The prism through which I viewed the world was a little distorted, I realize, but I couldn't help applying my perspective to what I saw. I was constantly having conversations in my head with these parents. They might have their experiences with their children cut short as well, so they should appreciate every minute.

Being in Hollywood I heard a lot of whining in general, and I had such a low threshold for that. I wanted to scream, "Are you kidding? Seriously?"

But I didn't. If we were at a party, I'd say, "Listen, Anthony, I will meet you in the car. Hurry up and say goodbye."

Then I'd sit in the car by myself while it took him an hour and a half to get out of there because he had to say goodbye to everyone for fear that he might hurt someone's feelings. I didn't care.

But I understood that Anthony had to network. He was sincere about it, and I think it was difficult for him to understand that oftentimes when people said, "Give me your number" or "Give me a call," that didn't mean they actually would respond.

It pained me so much to watch this happening. My feeling was, *Why would you mislead a person so sweet and so sincere that he believed you? He believed you!*

I didn't believe anything or anyone. I was thinking, *You know what? As soon as we leave the room, this person is going to engage in another conversation with someone else who might propel their career in some way.* I had grown very cynical. But I understood that I was still grieving and was depressed.

Plus, I was in a city that I didn't want to be in. For years I didn't want to be in LA.

Aside from all of the Hollywood phoniness and the absence of friends and family, there was this: In Chicago, at least the racism was overt. In Los Angeles it was subtle, real subtle.

"Did she just wait on that person before she waited on me?"

"Did they just ask them how they're doing and not ask me how I'm doing?"

"Did he just shake that person's hand and not my hand?"

This would happen at a party or business function or in a restaurant. It was like tiny drips on a rock that would erode my self-esteem or increase the risk of my becoming rageful. Anthony has a good spirit and is hardwired to be very forgiving, so he wasn't knocked back on his heels like I was. I'm a cynic at heart, so I'd tell him, "Watch out."

"Oh honey, please," he'd respond.

That's why we're so well balanced. Because while he was seeing this place as la-la-land, being Pollyannaish about certain things, I didn't have the time for that. His spirit is perfect for being out here in LA.

Mine is not.

Still, I stayed.

It was not worth breaking up our marriage just because I wanted to be back in Chicago with my family. I took my vows seriously. Literally and seriously.

But what we experienced put a lot of stress on our marriage.

Anthony

When Brigitte got upset with me, she wrote letters and left them on my pillow. I was right there at home, but instead of just telling me what was bothering her, she preferred to write a letter and put it on a pillow. I didn't understand that at all.

Brigitte

I didn't have a voice, I tell you. I was intimidated about sharing my feelings because as a child, I couldn't talk about them. "Who gives a damn about your feelings?" That was the language of my childhood home. So I felt the most appropriate way to get my needs across was to write a note.

A lot of our communication was nonverbal, and if you let that go on too long without a reality check, your perceptions can get distorted, and then this story line emerges in your head about the other person, fair or not. I felt like Anthony was withholding information or massaging the truth or lying and then trying to make me feel like I was crazy for whatever I was perceiving. I wasn't having it, but I also wasn't going to confront him.

These conflicts weren't about major issues. It's not like I suspected him of sneaking around or doing anything really destructive. It was just the little stuff that happens in a marriage, and sometimes you have to acknowledge what you did that hurt the other person. Maybe someone doesn't put down the toilet seat, and there's a big blowup. You know it's not about the toilet seat. It's about all of that unspoken stuff that you let build up.

Anthony

She said that I massage the truth or lie.

(I don't.)

Brigitte

Sometimes I played the Jewish mother card and said, "Before I die, can you at least tell me the truth? Before I take my last breath, can you at least acknowledge that you did A, B, or C?"

"No!"

Anthony

We were like zombies, but we also were in cocoons for all those years. We were cut off from each other and our own feelings. We couldn't spread our wings.

We hadn't grown them yet. There's a reason to be in a cocoon: to mature, to prepare for the coming transformation. We had to become stronger inside our shells. But in the meantime, at home, we were barely living.

Outside the house, I kept busy professionally as I tried to capitalize on my newfound exposure. Even though I was working with Buddy Morra plus an agent and, for a while, a publicist, I still had no grand career scheme. I wanted—and was getting—better stand-up bookings, but I also started angling for acting jobs. I felt boxed in as a comic.

One stumbling block was that I used to talk about my daughter onstage, but now she was gone, so I couldn't bring her up the way I previously had, and I wasn't about to get into what actually had happened. My comedy fed off my life experiences, but my life experiences no longer were conducive to comedy. That's how I looked at it, anyway—and I was determined not to share those aspects of my life in the first place. If I wasn't going to tell my friends, pastor, and manager about Brittany, I sure wasn't going to discuss her in front of crowds of strangers.

Instead of stretching myself as an artist, trying to channel those difficult emotions into my work, I leaned on the old bits. I didn't do anything dealing with having a child or being a parent. I filled those gaps with material that didn't hurt so much or cut so deep, jokes that were relatively silly. I'd gone from talking about being single to being married to having a baby to . . . now what?

So when, in my act, I appeared to be revealing things that were going on with me, that's when I felt like I was lying. I was riffing on regular, everyday stuff like this:

I'll tell anyone considering marriage in the near future, get to know the sleeping habits of that individual. Ask them directly: "Do you snore? Do you come from a snoring family? How should I wake you up once you start snoring?"

That would save you a lot of grief. I didn't do any of that. My wife snores. You ever sleep with somebody that snores so bad, they wake their own self up? Every night my wife is in bed going [makes loud snoring noises]. Then she taps me:

"I hear something."

"Oh, you think?"

I tried waking her up. I tried giving her wedgies. I tried smothering her. She just snores out her ears.

I wasn't digging into anything that reflected my ongoing feelings of loss, heartbreak, and the way those things change you and your relationships. The reason Richard Pryor, Bernie Mac, and George Carlin made me laugh was that they spoke the truth, daring to explore deep, dark parts of themselves. That's what my favorite comedians did.

But that's not was I was doing. I felt like a fraud.

One way to escape those feelings was to pursue acting. It's something I'd always wanted to do. When I was younger, stand-up seemed like an easier way of getting through the entertainment biz door, and it proved to be a more reliable way to make money, as crazy as that sounds. From the get-go, someone got labeled either as a comic or an actor because the assumption for a long time was that you couldn't do both. I was a comic.

Yet by 1991, there had been much crossover between the stand-up and acting worlds. Garry Shandling, whom I enjoyed seeing at the Comedy & Magic Club, had created and starred in *It's Garry Shandling's Show*, a groundbreaking sitcom that aired on Showtime from 1986 to 1990. He played a version of himself in this self-referential show that laid the groundwork for *Seinfeld*, an even more popular comedians' showcase that debuted in 1989 and ran for nine seasons.

I was far from that level. I went to acting auditions, and the first part I booked was on an episode of the Tony Danza sitcom *Who's the Boss?*, which aired in October 1991. I played Todd, not that you'd know my character's name without watching the end credits. I was one of several people seen sitting around a conference table while Judith Light's character, Angela, ran a meeting. I laughed a few times and joined a chorus of "And they called it puppy love . . . ," but, otherwise, I had no lines, at least not in the version that aired.

I learned that a sitcom's creative process was very fluid. The writers gave you a script in the morning, you did a table read with the entire cast, the writers revised the script, you read it again or conducted a full rehearsal, and it went back to them for more tweaking as they noted where the laughs didn't come or the performances weren't delivering. The show was all about precision, with everything needing to be nailed down. You did table reads Monday, directors blocked out the action with the cameras Tuesday, table reads for another episode took place Wednesday, that episode was blocked out Thursday, and both shows were taped Friday, with the script revisions continuing up to the moment when the cameras rolled. Everyone was professional and proficient.

I also acted in a pilot for a show starring comedian Paul Rodriguez. I had lines in that one and appeared in multiple scenes, so I was enthusiastic and told my family and friends. Then one Saturday someone from the show called me.

"Anthony, we went too long, and your scenes got cut."

"All of them?"

"Yes."

"My part isn't even going to be shown?"

"No."

They could do that? Just erase my entire part?

Yes, they could. This was Hollywood.

Lesson learned: Don't tell people when I shoot something. Don't say anything till it's ready to air or be released because explaining to everyone that my part got cut was too much trouble.

Another performance that never surfaced was my role in the pilot of the Farrah Fawcett–Ryan O'Neal sitcom *Good Sports*, which starred the real-life couple as coanchors of a cable sports show. I played one of the guys in the office, but by the time the show began its short run in 1991, my role had been axed.

In general when I was trying out for roles, I was in the category of clean-cut young black guys. When I entered a casting room, I saw a picture of Denzel Washington on the wall; he was the ideal. Later it was Laurence Fishburne or Will Smith. There was a pecking order for these guys, and I was far from the top. Also, as a six-foot-four guy, I wasn't going to get cast alongside the many Hollywood actors who were under six feet tall. I never could have been in a movie with Sylvester Stallone unless I was cast as the tall villain whom the shorter hero beats up.

When I went to audition for Mel Brooks's *Robin Hood: Men in Tights*, Mel told me, "No, no, you're too handsome." Couldn't he cast me on the basis of whether I was funny? Mel Brooks instead gave the role to a shorter young comedian making his film debut: Dave Chappelle.

I acted in an independent 1992 film called *The Windy City*, and the most notable aspect of that experience was that I was called upon to do an explicit love scene. The young woman acting opposite me didn't want to do it, and I didn't either, so I said, "We'll tell the director." He let us off the hook.

Later he hired another young woman who was willing to have her very curvy body exposed on-screen, and he cut the scene together to make it look like my hands were on her. When I was watching the movie at home with Brigitte and the woman lifted up her shirt to expose herself, Brigitte shot me such a look.

"I wasn't there," I protested. "Those aren't my hands."

The magic of movies.

Brigitte

The only time I got jealous in our marriage was when Anthony was filming that movie in Chicago. These were the days before cell phones, and I kept calling his hotel room and couldn't reach him. We recently had lost Brittany, and I was contending with a lot of aloneness, and I had a pang of jealousy. I did not like that feeling because I wasn't used to it.

I confronted him on it: "Why didn't you call? What's going on?" He was agitated that I kept asking.

I had to recognize this for what it was: my issue, not his. I squashed that quickly. Jealousy never was an issue between us after that.

Of course, then I saw the movie and what appeared to be his hands on that other woman's body, and I said, "Aw, hell, no."

Anthony

While my Hollywood acting career was off to a slow start, I still got work playing myself. Chuck Woolery, then famous for hosting the dating show *Love Connection*, had a talk show for a few months in 1991, and I was a guest on that. What I learned doing *The Chuck Woolery Show* was that my comedy works sitting down. The talent coordinators talk to you beforehand, feed questions to the host, and then you answer with your jokes. I had a blast and killed it too.

I was back on my feet for the *14th Annual Young Comedians Special*, which aired on HBO in December 1991. Richard Lewis, wearing all black, hosted with his usual eccentricity, and the lineup of up-and-comers included Drew Carey (almost four years before the debut of his self-titled sitcom), Jon Stewart (almost two years before he launched *The Jon Stewart Show* on MTV, three years before his movie debut in *Mixed Nuts*, and about seven years before he took over *The Daily Show*), Jeff Stilson (who would write for *The Late Show with David Letterman* and then write and produce for *The Chris Rock Show* and *The Osbornes*, winning Emmys for the last two), and Warren Hutcherson (who became a *Saturday Night Live* writer and writer-producer for *Living Single* and *The Bernie Mac Show*). By the time we taped the show at the Great American Music Hall in San Francisco, we all knew each other from working the clubs. I was closest to Drew Carey because he was another midwesterner, from Cleveland.

At the time this felt like just another gig rather than a special night. As always, I was completely in my own head, concentrating on my act and not paying attention to what anyone else was doing. I didn't watch the other sets, and I never even saw the show because I didn't have cable.

After it aired, people got me mixed up with Warren Hutcherson, the other black guy on the bill. He was very funny and had a routine about his father being in the Nation of Islam and seeing conspiracies in everything.

"Aren't you that funny Muslim?" they asked me.

"No, that was Warren Hutcherson."

As Warren and Jeff Stilson demonstrated, writing provided a viable career path for some comedians, but as I've mentioned, I'm not a writer per se. I work hard on my material but not by putting words to paper or onto a screen. I develop the routines in my head, repeating them over and over to get the jokes and phrasings exactly as I want them to be.

Phrasing is so important: Maybe I should say it this way; maybe I should structure it that way. I know what the joke is going to be, but where do I want to start it—the front, the back, or the middle? I might start a joke, "Yes, I did get arrested," and then back up. In the beginning I might think *this* was the joke, and the audience let me know that, no, the joke started here, or there—or there was no joke. Often I recorded my sets so I could listen to and study the audience reactions and thus learn about my own jokes.

At the Comedy & Magic Club, Jay Leno wrote a lot of stuff down to try out onstage, even saying, "Here's a new joke." A lot of times he wasn't testing whether the joke was funny so much as playing with how he phrased it. That's what I noticed about Garry Shandling, too, that he was always open to trying new material and would work it down to specific word choices and even how he would land on syllables.

Even though I didn't write out my routines, I did keep a notebook to track what worked and didn't work and also to jot down ideas in a sort of shorthand. People years later would ask me, "Remember when you used to do this joke?" and I'd say no. I didn't maintain any sort of archive for my material. But even now I could open a notebook onto a phrase or a single word I wrote down, and immediately I'd remember how it sparked a train of thought that led to a part of my act.

In general my jokes evolved by getting shorter. They started off long, and I trimmed and trimmed and trimmed. I looked at the geometry to find the straight line between two points. One thing I hated about Bill Cosby was he took all day to tell a joke. I would think, *Come on.* That was before I was even a comic.

Jay Leno took over *The Tonight Show* in May 1992, and he had me on that October. Appearing with Jay was different from appearing with Johnny Carson. Johnny was an icon, a legend, a guy I associated so strongly with television that seeing him in person was at first surreal. Jay was a guy I'd known for years.

Although I didn't get to open for Jay at Nashville's Zanies, we performed together other times. When he was at Zanies in Chicago, I was the emcee, a role at which I excelled because I kept everything running on time and didn't have the attitude *I'm going to blow out the headliner to prove that I should be the headliner.* After I moved to LA, Jay and I appeared together at the Comedy & Magic Club. I have pictures of us together that were taken decades apart.

Jay's a nice guy, really down-to-earth and not pretentious in any way. He loves stand-up and was taking outside comedy jobs even while he was hosting *The Tonight Show.* At the Comedy & Magic Club before his set, he'd sit in the greenroom, eating his chicken wings and french fries. I'd walk in—"Hey, Jay"—and he'd shoot the breeze until it was time to go on.

My stepfather never viewed my *Tonight Show* appearances as a big deal. He didn't think I'd made it even as his friends kept telling him, "But Fred, your son's on *The Tonight Show.*" He certainly didn't treat me any differently. When I visited home, I still had to empty the garbage, wash the dishes, and mow the lawn.

But my mom was thrilled about my TV success. She was my biggest fan, even if she didn't like all of my jokes. I would try them out on her, and she would say, "I don't think that's funny." Routines that I became known for— jokes that *killed*—prompted this reaction from her: "I don't get that."

But she was so proud of me and loved seeing me on TV. She flew out to Los Angeles to go with me to *The Tonight Show with Jay Leno.* The other guests that October 6 were actor Tom Skerritt and musician Michael Penn. Beforehand, my mom gave me instructions: "Don't point me out. Don't let people know who I am." She was insistent.

Then, lo and behold, she wore a big church hat and a pink and orange dress to the show. No one could miss her.

Brigitte

During a commercial break, Jay told Anthony's mama to stand up in the audience, and she got up and did a big wave. It was like she was Michelle Obama's mother or something.

Anthony

After the show wrapped up, Momma somehow got from the greenroom to the exit door, so as people were leaving, she stood there in her bright outfit, shaking hands and saying, "Hi. You know Anthony? That was my son up there!" It was hilarious. She got to meet Jay Leno as well, so she had a good day.

The second time I was on *The Tonight Show* with Jay, he got word that I was really sick with the flu, and one of his assistants doubted that I'd be able to rally to do my set. Jay himself came to my dressing room, where I was sitting in the dark with a fever of 104.

"Anthony, you look out of it," he said. "Are you okay? Can you pull this off?"

"Yes," I told him, and I did. I appreciated his personal touch in checking on me.

I also performed on *The Arsenio Hall Show* several times during that period when I was appearing on *The Tonight Show*. If you did *The Tonight Show*, you couldn't go on with David Letterman, and I never did. But it was okay to do Arsenio because that wasn't considered competition—in other words, it wasn't a show for white people. In the black world, being on with Arsenio was a bigger deal than doing *The Tonight Show*. I heard from more of my friends back home when I did Arsenio. A lot of brothers didn't watch *The Tonight Show*.

Again, I was going back and forth between the black and white worlds. Whites watched *Seinfeld*. We blacks watched *Martin*. Comedy was black and white, and I was somewhere in the middle. I could appeal to both sides, but that didn't get me to the top.

I missed out on the 1990s' biggest launching pad for black comedians: *Def Comedy Jam*, the HBO stand-up series hosted by Russell Simmons. Debuting in July 1992 and running till the beginning of 1997, this popular show provided huge career boosts to such African American comedians as Chris Tucker, Jamie Foxx, Cedric the Entertainer, Steve Harvey, Tracy Morgan, Kevin Hart, and my friend Bernie Mac. Because it was on cable television, with no language restrictions, the comics took full advantage to pepper their sets with profanities as they told explicit stories about sex and life in the hood.

I couldn't get booked on *Def Comedy Jam* because I wasn't dirty. I grew up in the community and knew how to make blacks laugh, but they said, "No, we want somebody who's raw, somebody who's hard-core."

So just as black comedy was reaching new heights, it was leaving me behind. But I received one indirect benefit from the rise of *Def Comedy Jam*. The show provided a huge stepping-stone for Bernie Mac, and he jumped from playing clubs to touring theaters that held three thousand to four thousand people. When his rocket shot up, he reached back and said, "Tony, you want to open up for me?"

"Sure."

I wondered how my style of comedy would mesh with his in-your-face attack. I was funny but knew I couldn't kill with that *Def Comedy Jam* audience like Bernie did.

"Tony, look," he said, "if you were dirty, I'd have to be dirtier. That wouldn't work."

So we went on tour together, hitting larger auditoriums than I'd ever played. It was during this tour, on a stop in Ohio, that my biological father reconnected with me. He apologized and took responsibility for his split with my mom, and he told me he had kept a scrapbook chronicling my career. He and I have never become close, but I appreciated all of this and forgave him.

Onstage I did my clean act, and then Bernie came out and declared, "Church is over, mother [bleep]ers!" People screamed in delight.

My first show with Bernie, the audience hated me. They actually booed. Bernie was the rare black comic who started on time. The show was scheduled to begin at 8:00 p.m., and I came on at 8:01. But the audience was trickling in at ten after, fifteen after, so they didn't hear my introduction, and my name wasn't on the marquee. Their reaction was, "Who is this brother, and why is he telling jokes?" All it took was one guy shouting "Where the [bleep] Bernie at?" before the audience was repeating it louder and louder: "Where the [bleep] Bernie at? Where the [bleep] Bernie at? Get the [bleep] off the stage."

It was funny to me that they were so mad that they were cussing. I didn't move. I didn't beg. Eventually I said, "If you shut up and let me perform, I can get offstage, and Bernie can come out."

Silence.

I did my thirty minutes and then introduced Bernie.

I was shaken, though, and talked to Bernie before the second show. Did I really want to do this?

"It's not that you're not funny," he told me. "You're just used to performing for whites. It's a different template."

I hadn't dressed the part, for one. When I came out in my plain black suit and started telling my jokes, the audience reacted: "Who is this guy? He's not us. He don't sound like us. He don't dress like us."

Here's another difference between the white and black comedy worlds. A white comedian can go out and perform without worrying about making a fashion statement. White comics or singers hit the stage in jeans and T-shirts, and the white audience is fine with that.

But blacks, we demand that you dress up and show some style. "Come on, man. I'm paying forty dollars for this ticket. You better not come out here in jeans."

The audiences practice what they preach, too, taking on an attitude of *We've got to get our flashy suits, got to get our dresses, got to get our shoes* because going to a concert is an event. During the late 1990s, when the Kings of Comedy tour starred Steve Harvey, D. L. Hughley, Cedric the Entertainer, and Bernie Mac, store owners made so much money because the fans in the seats wanted to appear as colorful as the performers onstage.

As I looked out at Bernie's audience, I saw people with a flashy sense of style. All the colors of the rainbow were in their garb. Some whites might have thought that they were dressed as pimps, drug dealers, and prostitutes. For my second show with Bernie, I decided to wear a pimp getup: a big, flashy, colorful outfit. I had to dress like that to identify with the audience and get the people to listen to me. Everything went better after that.

Still, once I finished my set, I ran to the back of the theater to hear the audience reactions:

"He was all right."
"He was boring."
"He was just different."

I was not what *Def Comedy Jam* had trained their audience to expect from a black comic. "You're not going to cuss or talk about being poor and black?" That still wasn't me. To thine own self be true.

White audiences had to adjust their expectations when they saw me too—for the same reason. *Def Comedy Jam* led them to believe that all black comics were blue.

Despite all of this activity, I remained on cruise control, not really enjoying anything. I was moving forward but not *pushing* forward. I was going with the flow. Was I less proactive with my career because I was grief-stricken? Maybe. I'm not sure I wanted anything that bad anymore. I didn't have that feeling of "I've got to get this!" Deep down, I didn't really care.

So I acted and told jokes onstage and then returned home to Brigitte's and my cocoon.

16

Pump the Brakes

I almost didn't marry my wife because she had the habit of walking into things when we were dating because she's farsighted, which I didn't know at the time because she never wore her glasses around me. I saw my wife walk into a brick wall once. Hard. I thought a car had backfired; that's how hard she walked into the wall. And she still refused to tell me she had an eye problem, even when she regained consciousness.

I'm like, "Baby, you okay?"

"Yeah, why you say that?"

"Because you just walked into that building."

"Well, I didn't see it."

"You didn't see the building? Exactly what part of the building didn't you see?"

"I didn't see the building. Are you calling me a liar?"

"No, I'm not calling you a liar. If you didn't see the building, you didn't see the building. In fact, now that I take a good look at the building, I can see how you missed it."

Brigitte

"You know, you two can always have more children."

That's what Anthony's mother said to us after Brittany passed away. I think she regretted it as soon as it came out of her mouth. This was a woman of wisdom. She didn't mean to be insensitive. She just didn't know what else to say. She had never lost a grandchild before. She was in the midst of her own grief.

I didn't hold it against her. But when someone loses a child, that's one thing you never say. It's not like a goldfish. You don't replace that child.

At the time, Anthony and I didn't discuss having another child. I couldn't do it.

I can't even have pets now. Not long after we lost Brittany, our cherished dog died of cancer. How did *that* happen?

I didn't want another pet to die. I didn't want another child to die.

Plus, I was really, really ill when I was pregnant with Brittany, and I couldn't go through that again. Even if Anthony wanted another child, I wasn't going to sacrifice myself to give him a baby. I didn't love him *that* much. That's how I felt after Brittany's death. I couldn't do it. I couldn't go through any of it.

Anthony

I didn't ask my wife whether she wanted to try to have another child. It would have devastated her if for any reason that child was lost. I still thought about the possibility though. I've never completely closed that door.

A couple at our church were struggling to have children. They'd done everything they could, including fertility treatments, but nothing was working. So they prayed. The wife told me she prayed to have two boys, and I wrote it down on my own prayer list.

Soon she had a boy, and she was so happy. I told her, "No, no, no. Your prayer was *two* boys." Brigitte likes to say I prophesied this.

Their *two* boys are now nineteen and eighteen, and when I see them, I think about what a gift they are because I knew how hard it had been for the parents.

For a while Brigitte wouldn't go to church because the pastor made such a big deal about Mother's Day. In a black church, all the mothers stand up to be acknowledged and are presented with flowers. If she participated, she'd have to answer questions she didn't want to answer, perhaps opening herself up to insensitive comments, such as "Don't worry; you'll have another." And if she stayed in her seat, that would be like denying a core part of herself.

Even though Brigitte and I weren't discussing children, other people constantly raised the subject. When I was at an audition, someone would ask, "Hey, do you have any kids?"

"No," I'd say, so we could move on.

Brigitte sometimes replied, "Not living," but that started a whole other conversation that neither side really wanted to have, so she stopped doing that. We went to great lengths to avoid discussing Brittany, especially with new acquaintances. But sometimes it was tough.

Brigitte

People asked all the time, "Do you have children?"

Anthony used to answer, "No," but as my grandmother would always say, "Once a parent, always a parent." I wasn't going to deny that I was a mother.

So I'd answer, "Yes."

But then people got really nosy.

"Really? How many?"

At this point Anthony and I were likely to reply with a joke. We wanted to distract them because we didn't want to get into it, and we didn't think, if they knew the whole story, that they would want us to either.

"Are you counting me as a child?" Anthony might say.

Or I'd jump in: "Well, you've got to count my husband too."

Ha-ha-ha-ha-ha—everyone would laugh, and we'd move on to another subject . . . we hoped.

But some people would not be deterred.

"No, seriously, how old is your—is it a girl or boy?"

We'd sigh. *Here we go. They are not ready for this story. They're just trying to be friendly, trying to get to know us, but they're digging.*

We attempted to redirect them, thinking, *They really don't want this,* but some people kept pushing. They were sincerely interested, but we wanted to stop it right then and there, just pump the brakes. They weren't picking up on the signals we were sending.

Instead, they were trying to add it all up: "You've been married so long and don't have kids?"

Plenty of couples don't have kids, either because they don't want to or because they can't. You have to be sensitive to either scenario; someone may be heartbroken over not being able to have children, and pushing the subject can be cruel. But not having kids goes against some folks' cultural grain. It's hard for them to compute.

"How many kids do you have? No seriously? How many?"

"One," we'd finally answer.

"Really? Only one? How come you haven't had any more?"

That's the question where we'd throw our hands up in the air. That's the one that made Anthony say, "They asked for it." At this point they deserved whatever we gave them.

So we'd tell the entire story.

By the end they'd be crying somewhere.

Anthony

After all that, we had to console *them.*

I'd be hugging them, saying, "It's okay. It's okay."

They were shook.

Brigitte

Yeah, they were shook. And their whole day was messed up.

As much as I opposed getting pregnant again, over time I softened to the idea of bringing another child into our lives. There were so many kids out there who needed a loving home. As someone who grew up in a home without love, I knew this—and I at least was able to live with a parent. Many children, often in difficult situations, didn't have even that.

So as the years went by, we discussed adoption. We agreed to adopt. We wanted to adopt. We *would* adopt. Eventually it no longer was a question.

17

One More Thing

"Hey, you're pretty tall. You play basketball?"

"No."

"You're pretty tall."

"I don't play though."

"Why? You're pretty tall."

"You're pretty short. You ride a horse?"

I don't like assumptions. Like whenever I'm in the grocery store, somebody might come up to me, "Excuse me, sir. Could you get that can off the top shelf for me?"

"Um, no. Why don't you eat what's on the second shelf? This is my stuff. That's your stuff."

Anthony

I was never a long-distance runner, but I kept in shape and tried to jog every day. One day when I was running, I noticed that my legs were getting numb. I thought I must not have warmed up properly. But it happened again—and again.

I decided to see a neurologist and did my research the old-fashioned way: I opened up the Yellow Pages. I found someone who looked like an expert and made an appointment.

When I went in, the office staff asked me, "Who's your doctor?"

"I don't have a doctor."

"Your family doctor is supposed to refer you to us."

"I cut through all that and found you."

Wasn't that a good thing?

The doctor examined me, putting probes on my head and body and measuring the electrical impulses. When he was done, he wouldn't give me the results.

"We'll tell your family doctor," he said.

"But I don't have a family doctor."

He still wouldn't discuss his findings with me, which seemed crazy, but okay: I got myself a family doctor, and the family doctor told me I needed to see a neurologist and referred me to a different one.

This neurologist put me through another battery of tests and did give me the results: I had a "mild" case of MS.

Multiple sclerosis is a degenerative disease that attacks the central nervous system: the brain and spinal cord. It basically causes the body's immune system to destroy the tissues protecting the brain's and spinal cord's nerve fibers, so "communication" among parts of your body becomes impaired, as do you. The disease is mysterious and unpredictable and has no cure. People can experience a lot of symptoms, then feel relief, then have a relapse, though the symptoms generally worsen over time.

I know now there's no such thing as mild MS. It's like telling someone she has a mild pregnancy. But because I was displaying few symptoms, the doctor didn't think I needed to start taking any medication or change my diet or, really, do anything differently. I think the medical world was in a different place regarding MS then than it is now.

In 1994, I found myself experiencing hand tremors. Dexterity was becoming a problem, and my voice was changing as well. I was never James Earl Jones—I was higher pitched, for one—but I did have a strong, commanding voice that popped. It had rhythm, swing, and snap to it, and it landed punch lines with impact. The voice is such a key element of comedy or any sort of acting. When I pretended to be my wife scolding me or my mom singing in church or gym-shoe-clad Ethiopians trying to catch a cheetah, my voice took on various pitches and volumes to make you believe I was embodying those characters.

Now my speech was slowing down, my pitch getting lower, developing more of a burr and a shakiness. If I started out as Chris Rock, I was moving in the direction of the Jimmy Stewart you'd see on *The Tonight Show* in the 1970s.

The doctor performed more tests, including an MRI, and put me on a medicine, Copaxone, which works to reduce the frequency of MS relapses, though it doesn't necessarily stymie the disease's progression. I started occupational therapy and was given exercises to keep my hands flexible. I used a grip strengthener and manipulated golf balls in my hands, both of which I still do. Because I was struggling with my pincer grasp—that's what babies learn so they can pick up little objects like Cheerios between the thumb and index finger—the therapists suggested that writing with a heavier pen would reduce the tremors. I was grateful that I didn't have to do too much writing since I still was composing my comedy routines in my head.

So much remains unknown about MS, including how you contract it. One theory is that it's dormant in your system until a trauma brings it to the forefront. With me that certainly was a possibility.

Brigitte

The first things I noticed were the changes in Anthony's voice and dexterity. He also struggled to come up with words; he'd describe the function of an object instead of the object itself. Over time his vocabulary choices became so different from what they had been.

As the years went by, I started to fill in the blanks for him, to feed him the right words, until one of the doctors told me, "You've got to stop doing that. You've got to let him do the cerebral work."

With MS there's also some agitation and irritability, so if he was fumbling for a word and I was making him work for it, he would say, "Why can't you just give me the word? Come on. Give me the word."

But I wasn't benefiting him by being his second brain. He could be very resistant and hardheaded. If I said, "Up," he might say, "Down," just to assert himself.

He also may not have appreciated the "mommy" tone I took with him. "Anthony, why are you putting on your pants standing up? Shouldn't you be sitting down?" No adult wants to be asked that. But I knew what would happen if he fell. I'm the one who would have had to take him to the hospital, all because he wouldn't sit down to put on his pants. But he felt like I was violating his independence, even when he was doing stuff that was not in his best interest.

Anthony

I had to stop playing basketball with my friends because I could no longer shoot the ball well. I didn't offer any explanation. One day I simply announced, "This is the last time I'm playing."

My friends were confused.

"What? Your wife won't let you play anymore?" they asked.

I laughed but told them nothing. As with so many aspects of my personal life, I remained closemouthed. I wouldn't share. I was bottling up more and more. I wouldn't give them the real story, so they came up with their own.

I kept this news quiet in professional circles too. I was starting to get some traction, landing some movie roles. The people who cast me couldn't tell I had MS. No one could at that point. So I proceeded like a young guy whose star was on the rise.

Brigitte

For those first several years, he was pretty good at hiding his condition.

But once Anthony was diagnosed with MS, that ended the adoption discussion. We had enough challenges on our plate. I longed to give children the kind of love that I never experienced, but I'd have to find another way.

Anthony

I was portraying Malcolm X in a play, *The Meeting*, when I auditioned with director Mario Van Peebles for his movie *Panther*, about the Black Panther Party's community work and conflicts with Oakland police in the late 1960s. Having grown up being served breakfast by them, I thought the Black Panthers were from Chicago, but I learned that was just a chapter of the Oakland-based organization. Playing Malcolm X, I was in a militant state of mind, with a goatee to match, when I auditioned for the role of activist Stokely Carmichael. At the end of my second audition, I was told, "Don't shave, and don't cut your hair."

I didn't hear anything for several weeks but followed their instructions. I hadn't mentioned the audition to any of my friends, so when they saw me looking increasingly scraggly with my expanding Afro and goatee, they thought, *What's going on with Anthony?* Maybe I was getting high, or Brigitte had kicked me out of the house, and I was semi-homeless. As I would learn over and over, if you don't tell people the real story, they'll come up with their own.

When the play's run ended, I returned to doing stand-up, and Budd Friedman invited Brigitte and me to Puerto Rico so I could help him launch his new Improv club there. Right before we left, I got the call: I'd been cast in *Panther* as Eldridge Cleaver, the militant party leader and author of *Soul on Ice*. At first I was annoyed because I'd auditioned to play Stokely Carmichael. Little did I know that Mario Van Peebles had decided to play Stokely Carmichael himself—and that Eldridge Cleaver was the meatier role.

I studied tapes of Eldridge Cleaver to get down the way he talked, appeared, and acted, and the movie folks gave me contact lenses to lighten my eyes from brown to hazel. Once I arrived on set, people kept telling me I looked just like him. In fact, while we were filming in Oakland, a guy came up to me and said I still owed him money. I had to argue with him: "Dude, I'm the actor. I'm not the real guy."

Not a lot of Hollywood movies at the time were being made with such large black ensembles, and by the end we felt like we were a family doing something special. The cast included several performers who were or would become prominent: Courtney B. Vance, who played Bobby Seale and went on to win an Emmy for playing Johnnie Cochran in *The People v. O. J. Simpson: American Crime Story*; Angela Bassett, fresh off her Oscar-nominated performance in *What's Love Got to Do with It*, in the small part of Dr. Betty Shabazz (she married Courtney B. Vance a couple of years later and also has the distinction of having acted in *Panther* and *Black Panther*); comedian/activist Dick Gregory, who played Reverend Slocum; rapper Kool Moe Dee, who played a character named Jamal; and Chris Rock, who had the small role of Yuck Mouth.

Then there was the actor who played "Bodyguard," basically an extra who shouted "Right on, brother!" in the background as Bobby Seale and Eldridge Cleaver argued over whether the Panthers' protests should be peaceful or violent. This guy kept getting louder and louder, and when Bobby Seale finally cut him off, I couldn't tell whether that was the character or Courtney B. Vance getting mad at him. I had to keep myself from laughing. If I had to predict who in the cast someday would collect $25 million for a movie, I would not have guessed "Bodyguard," aka Chris Tucker.

My role was a straight-up dramatic one, no comedy involved. Having just performed in *The Meeting* helped because that was in a small black box theater, so my acting had to be scaled down, as it is on film, as opposed to my having to project to the balcony. A lot of major theater actors have trouble transitioning to film or TV because they're too big in their acting. When I auditioned for *Panther*, Mario Van Peebles probably saw a guy who had a stillness about him. But I was still learning.

One challenge was having to memorize a script, in this case one written by the director's father, Melvin Van Peebles, himself a veteran filmmaker. I had to drop a lot of f-bombs, which was out of my comfort zone. I was glad to be wearing sunglasses so you couldn't see the bashfulness in my eyes.

But to me if you're playing someone historical, you can't clean them up. When I played Malcolm X, was I supposed to make him a Christian? In my work I need to be true to the characters, to honor the scripts. I wasn't seeking fictional roles in which I cussed a lot and misused women. I have an internal moral compass. But I will honor historical characters. If you filmed the story of Jesus, not everybody could play Jesus. Somebody has to play the Romans, the disciples, the Jewish people, and everyone else.

The Bible is full of people who struggled internally and externally. They were dealing with rage, depression, suicidal thoughts—no one is perfect. That's why the Bible resonates with me. When I look at these founders of the faith, I see flawed individuals who experienced life and all of its battles. And that's what attracts me to acting: to get inside the skin of flawed people and understand their struggles.

Acting on film also made me nervous in that I had to say the lines the same way with my body in the same position each time. I had to be consistent from take to take so the director could cut together a coherent performance.

I learned that acting for the cameras is more technical than emotional.

Even more so on a scripted project than on a talk show, you have to hit this mark because that camera is watching you, and these lights are hitting you at a certain place. If you miss the mark, then you throw off the lighting as well as the camera operator because you're not looking where you're supposed to look. If you pick up a cup of coffee in take 1, you must pick it up the same way in take 35; otherwise, the editor can't match the takes. As an actor, you want to do something a bit differently each time to keep it fresh, but nope. That's why acting on camera can get boring for actors. It's not like acting onstage, where everything stays live and new.

It's like a football team when the quarterback throws the ball to where you're supposed to be; everyone must be in sync all the time. To be able to perform at that level takes great concentration, yet you also must be comfortable because any conscious effort will show.

Brigitte

Anthony said the director told him, "Man, you look just like Eldridge Cleaver. I hope you have the chops." I wondered, *Does he have the chops?* I didn't know.

When I finally saw Anthony in *Panther*, I thought, *Whoa.* He wasn't even recognizable to me because he was a mean guy in that movie compared to the guy I know. That's when it struck me that he was more of a dramatic actor than a comedic actor. When he was on sitcoms and was supposed to be funny, that never worked as much for me. His dramatic bent always resonated more. Even in comedies, such as *Curb Your Enthusiasm* that he did years later, he was funnier when he played it straight.

Anthony

While we were filming *Panther*, I thought, *Oh man. We're making a big movie.* For some reason, though, when it came out, it did not get much hype or heat. Maybe the powers that be thought the movie might cause blacks to revolt. Or maybe this was more evidence of the struggles of serious black dramas to attract audiences. Either way I was expecting *Panther* to be huge, and it was not. What you think will be big doesn't pan out, yet something for which you have low expectations might become a hit.

Although I was swearing on-screen in a role that was a huge departure from my onstage persona, I didn't get any blowback. Over my entire career, I think I've had only one person who said, "Shame on you." My parents didn't. My pastor didn't. This person had seen *Panther* and emailed my website to say, "We can no longer support you."

I was like, *Okay, bye.*

My mom was excited to see me portraying Eldridge Cleaver. For one, that was her baby on-screen, and her children could do no wrong. But also she was a part of the '60s and that revolutionary movement. For me to play someone who was pivotal in that movement was exciting to her. She knew that wasn't her Tony behaving in such a way. She knew that when I came home, I wasn't cussing or acting like Eldridge Cleaver. She was fine with it. So were my pastor and the people I respected the most. They understand the frailty of people and being true to historical figures.

One job leads to another, and that's how I got *Tales from the Hood*, which had the same casting director. This black-themed horror anthology was directed by Rusty Cundieff, and I was in the first of the movie's four tales, playing Clarence, a police officer who watches his white partner and other cops brutally assault—and later kill—a black activist. A year later a broken-down Clarence, following orders from the murder victim's ghost, lures the perpetrators to a cemetery for some supernatural justice.

I learned another important technical lesson on this set. I cry easily, so I nailed it when I had to do so on camera.

"Great take, Anthony," the director said. "We're gonna do it again."

My problem was that I really was crying, letting it all out, and you can't sustain that kind of energy and emotion by take 12. An acting teacher had to show me how to fake cry so people don't know that you're faking.

"If you really cry, you're not servicing the character," the teacher told me. "You're servicing you, Anthony."

I didn't learn stuff like that in college.

Much of my *Tales from the Hood* segment was shot in a cemetery, and I'd get sleepy on the set. There was a coffin rigged up there, so sometimes I lay down in it to take a nap.

"How can you sleep there?" people asked.

"Easy," I said. "I'm tired, and it's quiet."

Panther opened May 3, 1995, and *Tales from the Hood* opened three weeks later. *Tales* wasn't a huge hit but made almost twice as much as *Panther*, and in the black community it became a cult classic. When I went to the barbershop, people gave me a curious look before saying, "Clarence, Clarence." The brothers loved *Tales from the Hood* because it was funny and scary, the same reason they loved *Get Out* years later.

Some people in Chicago had trouble believing that someone they grew up with was now on the big screen. My stepfather's reaction was to think that gave him the right to enter the theater without a ticket.

"Fred, you've still got to pay," my mom told him.

"Why I gotta pay to see Tony?"

"You can't just walk into the movie theater and say, 'That's my son.' It doesn't work like that."

With two movies out in a month plus appearances on *Arsenio* and other shows to promote them, I was as hot as I'd ever been.

I didn't act in another movie or TV show for two years.

18

Finding Our Voices

If we get into a disagreement, she goes, "Well, if I do that, how would that make you feel?"

I say, "Hey, hey, c'mon. If we're going to argue, we're going to argue like husband and wife: I'm going to yell at you, you're going to throw stuff and call the police—you know, like regular people."

Brigitte

Anthony had a mistress. I realized that early in our marriage. The mistress was comedy, and I was always going to come in second.

I had to ask myself whether I was willing to stay in a relationship knowing that I would be given second best. I decided I would. However, as the years passed by, I also realized that I had to take care of myself, which meant I had to find my own voice.

Once when I was traveling with Anthony, I realized I was starting to enjoy myself. This was a rare occurrence after Brittany's death, but when I mentioned it to my aunt, she said, "What about you?" I didn't understand the question, so she repeated, "What about *you*? What if something happened to Anthony? Where are you in this?"

I started to internalize. *Where is my identity?* Before that I had identified myself as a mother and a wife, never as Bridge or Brigitte. I was somewhat wounded that my aunt was not allowing me to bask in the enjoyment of my husband. But I also thought, *What do I need to do for* me?

I set aside my irritation and allowed God and the universe to lead me. I started becoming more interested in doing things without Anthony. It was liberating.

I took a photography class at one of the local colleges and found that my main interests were children and woundedness. Brittany was the conduit for everything. Whether it was photography or a basket-weaving class, she was always in there. Her voice was with me as I learned how to work a 35mm camera, and she was in the lens as well. Through photography I tried to capture in the most tangible ways my thoughts and feelings of the moment. If I was feeling sad or a baby's cry had triggered me or I saw a chunky little infant with those fat folds, I would take pictures. That was my journal. It was cathartic.

The next thing you know, I was okay with not going on the road with Anthony and not going to movie premieres with him. I didn't feel alone. I wasn't basking in my sorrows. I was allowing the grief process to play out as I nudged myself forward. Pursuing my own interests prompted me to get out of the fetal position at long last.

Even when I was in pain, I found comfort in my daughter. I thought, *Brittany had pain. How would she have dealt with this? She wouldn't have complained.*

Now I needed a vocation that was different from Anthony's. It was time for me to do my own thing, to take a journey that was not contingent upon him making money.

Especially because he was cooling off.

Anthony

I don't know why I got fewer roles after *Tales from the Hood*. The MS may have been a factor, as well as my overall energy level and lack of drive after Brittany died. I lost my momentum during that ten-year period after she passed away. The hunger wasn't there like it was when I first arrived in Los Angeles. Even though I never stopped working, I also couldn't shake myself out of that depressive fog. Secretly battling multiple sclerosis didn't help.

Part of what was happening was the natural order of things in Hollywood. I was now in my midthirties and no longer a fresh face. Younger versions of myself were coming up in the clubs as well as moving into film and television. I enjoyed the snowball effect of doing *The Tonight Show* and *The Arsenio Hall Show*, *Panther* and *Tales from the Hood*, but Hollywood is fickle. Work begets work, and when you land something, you're in demand, but then if you don't work for a while, you're less desirable. Once you're out, it's hard to get back in. Hollywood keeps rolling forward whether you're on board or not.

I never had a three-year plan or a five-year plan. I have a one-day plan. Back then it was a one-gig-at-a-time plan.

Sometimes things worked out. In 1997 my agent called to say, "Anthony, we have an offer for *Savannah*."

"When do I audition?"

"No, you don't have to audition. You have the role."

Savannah was a TV drama produced by Aaron Spelling, whose *Beverly Hills, 90210* also was on the air at that time. In Aaron Spelling's shows, everybody was good-looking: the women were pretty, and the guys all had six-packs. For my three episodes, I played a bad guy named Bill Webber, also known as Mr. Bill. I had a showdown with one handsome man, and in my third episode I got beaten up by one of the women. She was about five feet four and came up to my chest. *Really?* I thought. *You chose her to beat me up?* They had to choreograph it where I went down so she could kick me.

I also appeared in a movie that year called *Steel Sharks*, which was kind of a low-budget *Crimson Tide* starring Gary Busey and Billy Dee Williams. Gary Busey was always late, and when he hadn't made it onto the set for a scene that he and I were supposed to do together, I had to deliver all of my lines to a marker on the wall. He finally showed up at the end of the day, and I had to do the scene again off camera so he could look to the right spot while he did his part. Everything was cut together later. *Steel Sharks* never got a US release.

When my manager, Buddy Morra, retired in the late '90s, I was handed off to some other people at his firm, but it was never the same. Buddy was the one who had gotten me on *The Tonight Show* and made such a personal investment in me. Now I was just another guy in a firm's talent stable, and they had hotter performers to promote, ones who weren't in that no-man's-land between comedian and dramatic actor.

The agent is trying to get to the next level. The manager is trying to get to the next level. The casting directors are trying to get to the next level. Everybody is hustling. No job in Hollywood is safe. It's hard to get into the business, it's hard to stay in the business, and it's hard to enjoy the business because you're always looking for work. When I got a job, I was happy, but once that gig was up, I was back in line, auditioning for another one, never stopping to relax and enjoy the little victories.

In Hollywood what you shoot today might not come out for another two years, if at all, and during that time you still need to make money. If you're a comic or singer, you can do shows while waiting for those bigger projects to see the light of day, but taking live gigs complicates things further.

Although stand-up was seen as being part of New York's cultural scene, in Hollywood unless you were making a movie or TV show, you might as well have been starving. Your managers and agents didn't want you taking out-of-town gigs because out of sight, out of mind—and they wanted you available if something came up. If they weren't getting you into movies or onto TV shows, they weren't making much money from you (or for you).

"You've got to be here," they said.

Working auditions into your comedy-gig schedule is tough anyway. Auditions keep you on hold for so much time, like a plane sitting on the runway awaiting takeoff. Sometimes I was on the road when I got the call that I had an audition, so I broke it to the club owner that I had to leave.

"But you're supposed to work here till the end of the week."

"I've got to get back."

"Okay, you won't work here anytime again."

I'd think, *That's okay. I'm going to be a star.* Then I'd get back to town and find out that the audition was canceled.

When I did audition, there were so many reasons I might not get a role: too tall, not black enough. I heard that last one several times and responded, "Oh, you mean I'm not *street* enough. That's not the same as black." Then I thought, *I'm definitely not getting this role because I just told the casting director what "black" is.*

At various points agents and managers told me, "We don't know what to do with you, so we're going to let you go." Brigitte got angry at that, arguing that the manager or agent wanted the money but didn't want to work hard for it. Back in old Hollywood, those representatives cultivated artists, but today the burden is more on you, the actor; these days you must develop a social media following and things like that. When we met potential managers, Brigitte said, "If we've got to do all the work, then why do we need you? If we need to figure out how to keep his career going, then you're not the agent or manager for us."

So I cooled off in Hollywood. I wasn't on TV or film, so I was nobody. As I battled with myself and my representatives, I thought, *Maybe it is over.*

Then I was back onstage, and people were laughing, and I thought, *I do have a skill.*

If I could offer any advice to my younger self or others arriving in Hollywood, it would be to maintain a passion for something other than your work to balance yourself. Hollywood says you've got to focus totally on the business because it's all or nothing, yet success is so fleeting. Have balance in your life. If you fall in love, fall in love, and if you're an artist, that will enhance your art.

Being married, that was my balance—because Brigitte demands a balance. She *is* the balance.

But there was friction with her too.

Brigitte

I asked him, "Don't you want more?"

"No," he said.

"Mediocrity is okay for you?"

"I don't consider it mediocrity."

To an extent Anthony's rise was thwarted by his illness. At the same time, I didn't think he was trying to be the best he could be. I communicated my disappointment in his thought process. I thought he was settling. There were many ways he could have built on what he was learning, but he wasn't interested.

Anthony

Many of my colleagues found success working behind the scenes on late-night shows, sitcoms, *The Simpsons*, or other projects, but that's not how I viewed myself or my skill set. Writing for a sitcom required muscles that I lacked— and not just those required to actually write things down.

Comics who write for sitcoms must set their egos aside, and I'm not sure I could do that. I would get bored writing material for the same characters week after week, and I might get that feeling of *I'm supposed to make your show better when I should be doing my own show.* Comics are always thinking, *Well, it shouldn't be this way; it should be that way, and if it were my show, that's how I would do it.*

My friend Paul Feig solved this problem by creating the TV series *Freaks and Geeks* before going on to direct the movies *Bridesmaids*, *Spy*, and the *Ghostbusters* remake. But that wasn't my path.

Brigitte

There were something like twenty or thirty comics who came out to LA in the same decade as Tony and ended up becoming writers, directors, producers, and showrunners. Even though stand-up was in their blood, they also saw the financial and creative upsides to transitioning into these other areas. Paul Feig was one. Joey Gutierrez and Diane Burroughs, who together wrote on *Martin* and were writer/producers on *The Drew Carey Show* and *Still Standing*, were two others. It's easy to forget that John Ridley, who wrote *Three Kings* and won an Oscar for *12 Years a Slave* and created the series *American Crime*, started out in stand-up.

The successful people moved forward, and the next chapters of their careers usually involved working behind the scenes. But that's not what Anthony wanted to do.

If you see comics who after many years are still doing the clubs, for relative pennies, that means either they're not married or they can't find any other avenues for their work, and they may be facing financial challenges. Anthony obviously wasn't in the first category, and I didn't want the other two to apply to him either. They didn't really—he had raised the bar for himself higher than that.

But we weren't well-off. And Anthony was joking about it.

> I got so many bill collectors after me, when they come to my house, they carpool. I hate bill collectors. They're always calling me up, trying to get their money back. I'm like, "Hey, man, *you* preapproved *me*. I knew I didn't have any money."

> They're always calling my house.
> "Can I speak to Anthony Griffith?"
> "He's not in."
> "When do you expect him back?"
> "As soon as you hang up."
> Their latest tactic is to leave messages on your answering machine like they're your boy. I'll go home, I'll check my machine, and I'll hear: "Griff, what's up, dog? Give a brother a call, man. I'll try and hook up with you. I'm at 1-800 . . ."

Of all of his comedy routines, that's the only one that embarrassed me. I didn't like that people got the impression that we couldn't pay our bills. That wasn't the case, and there weren't a lot of bill collectors. I do remember that he missed one payment on his Sears card, and they sent it to a collection agency, and even when he tried to pay it, they were threatening him and his credit. He was offended.

"I've been with you guys for twenty years, and you treat me like this?" he said.

I was like, *Ooh, that's my man.* I thought it was sexy when he actually stood up for himself. He thought loyalty was paramount.

Too much of the time, though, I thought he lacked assertiveness. He was more passive than I wanted him to be. He's not a diva, and he wasn't going to give anybody a hard time, but he needed to move on from some professional relationships that weren't doing much for him anymore. Anybody in the industry would tell you that Anthony is a nice guy. If someone ever told you that Anthony had cursed somebody out, you'd say, "No, you must not be talking about Anthony Griffith." He's known as a sweet, quiet guy, but that only gets you so far when you don't speak up for yourself. Nice is seen as a weakness, and he always said yes to things, even if they weren't going to help his career.

Anthony

I was brought up to say "Yes," "May I?" and "Thank you." I didn't think I was weak just because I was nice.

Brigitte

Anthony's career was stalling, and we were struggling. There's nothing worse than a dream deferred, and I did not want to be the one to put sand in his tank. I didn't want to be that person. I wanted to live up to the stereotype of the strong black woman who supports her man no matter what. And I thought if we could survive Brittany's death, then everything else was just a little incidental issue.

At the same time, you've got to know when to hold them and when to fold them. I had come out to LA for him, but I wasn't going to sit back like a martyr and watch him wait for the phone to ring. Then it really would have been over because I would have given him all the keys to the toolbox that he wasn't using.

I knew that I had to individuate from him. That meant I had to allow him to be taken advantage of to some extent because I'd been spending too much energy trying to convince him that he shouldn't fall victim to the ways some club owners continued to exploit him. When he was out on the road, it drove me crazy how he was treated, yet I had to let go of all that. I didn't travel with him much anymore, but he wasn't going to stop touring, and I understood that, though I didn't like it. I thought, *He's not giving up* his *gig. Now I've got to find something that makes me happy and is a passion.*

I wanted to work in a helping profession. My mother always dropped references about my becoming a psychiatrist because, as she put it, there were always a lot of crazy people around. She knew all about that. I wasn't open to receiving guidance from her, but she had picked up on something about my temperament and personality, and a nugget of that suggestion stuck, consciously or subconsciously.

I wasn't sure what kind of position or degree I would pursue, and I had no concept of categories and specialties. But I knew that I welled up with emotion whenever I was around someone who had experienced trauma or sadness or who had been bullied. My heart was easily filled, and I understood this reaction came from my own experiences growing up as well as what we'd gone through with Brittany. I had become hypersensitive to other people's pain.

I needed to go back to school, so I enrolled in the premed program at UCLA, basically following my mom's advice. But the quickest way to get me to kiss the ground is for me to see blood. I was able to handle it with Brittany, but for whatever reason, when I see blood from anyone else, I lose it, so medical school was a tough fit. Also, I was most interested in conducting therapy, and it would've taken me a long time to get to that part while pursuing an MD. I didn't want to go through all that. I wanted to become a psychologist, not a psychiatrist, so I changed my track.

I felt like Anthony should be as supportive of my career choices as I had been of his. But from my perspective, that was not the case.

Anthony

I made the mistake of asking her, "How long is this going to take? How many classes will there be?"

"Education is forever," she said.

Well, what does that mean financially?

Brigitte

I think it was overwhelming for him to consider what I was doing. It was like, *Wow, that's a lot of school.*

But for years I'd wanted to ask him, "How many acting classes are you going to take?" He'd been taking them since I'd known him. My classes were going to result in a degree and a profession. When would his pay off?

I had to sit back almost passively and not have input into what his trajectory would look like because it was his passion. As wives, we can be hesitant about speaking our minds because we don't want to become a barrier to our spouses' vision. *How long is this going to take? How many auditions do you have to go on?* We don't want to ask those types of questions, but we think them.

So although he wasn't meaning to be malicious, he was circumventing my dream by asking me, "How long is this going to take? How many classes?" He had his voice in our relationship, and I was still trying to get mine. My thought bubble was: *Here's the mirror. Now, can you reflect those questions back to yourself?* But I didn't have the guts to say it. Even though I was supportive, I felt like I had no say-so in how he was going to proceed with his journey, but he had a say-so in how I would proceed with mine.

Anthony

For a long time I was not making a lot of money for the family. I did put Brigitte through a lot. I was the struggling artist and, I guess, self-centered because I was thinking, *Hey, I got a little gig. What's the problem?* She looked at it like, *At what point do you say it didn't work?* She finally asked me, "How long are you going to give it a shot before you realize that maybe this isn't meant to be?"

I was very irritated at that. *What do you mean, stop this?*

"Why don't you get a day job?" she asked. "Get a real job. Forget this fantasy. You didn't make it."

That's a hard pill to swallow for a creative person.

I had a job, and I worked hard at it.

The occasional role still popped up. Bernie Mac, for whom I still sometimes opened, gave me a small guest spot on his sitcom, *The Bernie Mac Show* (in an episode written by Warren Hutcherson, with whom I'd performed more than a decade earlier on the *14th Annual Young Comedians Special*), and one day called me to ask, "Is your SAG [Screen Actors Guild] card up to date?"

"Yes."

"You're gonna get a call in about ten minutes from the casting agent of *Charlie's Angels*."

Sure enough, ten minutes later the casting director for *Charlie's Angels: Full Throttle*, the sequel to the 2000 hit *Charlie's Angels*, called me and said, "We have a part for you."

That came directly from Bernie. I had only a couple of scenes, and some of my work got cut, but it was a fun, high-profile job. Bernie was Bosley, the Angels' boss, and I played one of his two cousins. Bernie had his own trailer, so I hung out in there with him.

I understood that I wasn't the man, but that was okay. I'm not someone who gets jealous. I've never said, "Oh, I wish I could be like Will Smith." I sort of like having my anonymity. I'm cool. Maybe in Hollywood you need more of that competitive feeling: *I'm going to beat him.* You need to push the people who represent you: "Come on, man. I've got to get in there for that audition."

I guess I never saw myself as a movie star, after all. I'd already come a long way from Chicago's South Side. My vision wasn't that big. I'd love to have that fame and fortune, but I was an okay actor, and to become a big deal, you must perfect what you're doing. Too many people are competing against you for you to be just okay.

But comics can make a living and have a life without being famous. If you decide that you don't need to be a star, you can be at peace and focus on the work that you have.

I enjoyed a whole side career as an opening act for noncomics. I was a hired gun: "He's going to make people laugh. He's clean." I toured briefly with Ben Vereen, who was doing his song and dance. When I came to Hollywood, he was one of the first guys I saw auditioning. I thought, *This is weird. That's Chicken George from* Roots. *He shouldn't be auditioning for the same role that I'm auditioning for.* That's when I became aware that people in Hollywood don't necessarily know what they want. They need a black guy? That may mean a black guy from thirty to sixty years old. I don't think either one of us got the part. Years later, when I opened for him, he was really nice. He always watched me from the wings.

I did a one-off with Kenny G and another one with Roberta Flack; a friend asked me to get her to sign some albums, which she did and was nice about it. I opened for Al Jarreau for a weekend in Las Vegas, and I have a picture of me with Ray Charles from another gig in Atlantic City. When I was in Philadelphia, doing a run of comedy club shows, I was asked to open for Donna Summer at a nearby gig. Brigitte was with me: "You're performing with who?" She went for the headliner but still got nervous beforehand that people might boo me. They didn't; the shows went great.

I got tabbed to open for James Brown at the Greek Theatre in LA, and before I went on, his people said, "We don't know where James is, so just stay onstage until we give you the light."

I performed for about thirty minutes and went over well, even though everyone was itching for the funk. Then James Brown's musicians and dancers came on and did their thing while waiting for him to show up. By the time JB hit the stage, he had about twenty minutes to perform because of the theater's curfew. The audience was annoyed—but not at me.

When the Temptations played West Coast gigs, they often called me to open, and I met them at the hotel or venue. Sometimes we performed in the inner city for an African American audience, and sometimes we played for a whiter audience, and the Temptations didn't have to change what they did from place to place because they had such broad appeal. I thought, *Hey, they don't have to switch up, and I don't have to switch up.* I felt like my comedy was universal as well. I enjoyed being with them. They were always changing their clothes. They dressed up, so I dressed up, and we worked well together.

Brigitte

I pulled back from Anthony's career so I could concentrate on my own, hunkering down to work on my PsyD at the California School of Professional Psychology. I wanted the highest degree possible, and I wanted to do it in four years even though they told me it would take five. I was too old to spend that long in school.

"I'm doing it in four years, whatever it takes," I said.

And I did, though it was a big sacrifice of my time and social life. My friends didn't know how to deal with it, and some didn't understand why an African American woman was seeking to become a doctor of psychology.

But soon enough I was walking across the stage to receive my doctorate. My husband was there, and so were my grandmother and other relatives. I would always be a wife and a mother, but now I was something else: Dr. Brigitte Travis-Griffin.

I had been arrested in my emotional development. I went back to graduate school in my forties, but once I found my voice and put on my skates, I went from zero to ten and didn't look back.

Anthony

I was ecstatic. When Brigitte came down to the garage to drive to the ceremony, she found that I had decorated her car with bells, cans, and party stuff and written on the rear window and side of the car, "Just Graduated." She was shocked.

This was a milestone. Everyone knew she was going to school. All the comics had heard about it. We all were happy because we knew how hard she had worked. It was like being able to brag about a kid who had graduated. I did that with Brigitte. Like college kids, we had spent a lot of evenings eating ramen noodles.

This was an example of Brigitte coming up with a plan and sticking to it no matter what. There were details of her plan that I didn't even know about.

For years we had had mismatched furniture. "I do not want this," she said. "I don't want us to look like we're still in college."

Later I saw that Brigitte had made a scrapbook filled with pictures showing how she wanted the house to look when she graduated. She also decided how much money she would make once she started to practice, and she stood firm.

"That's a bit too high," her colleagues said. "When you get out of school, if you get a salary that's this amount, you should be happy."

"No, I'm going to ask for at least double that," Brigitte said.

"You're crazy."

But her plan came to fruition. Her standards were and remain extremely high.

Brigitte

Some things changed at home. I quit leaving notes on pillows. I spoke up, told Anthony what was on my mind, and tried to root out any problems instead of avoiding them the way I had for so much of my life.

"You're therapizing me," Anthony said.

I didn't think I was, but it was a paradigm shift.

Anthony

When Brigitte started studying psychology, it was so obvious that she was trying to do therapy on me at home. I was like, *Really?*

Brigitte

How I engaged with Anthony before going to graduate school was less mature than it was now that I had my degree. Through my studies I developed a different language, a different way of communicating. Instead of walking on eggshells or losing my temper, I could listen to and reflect on what he said. He saw that as trying to conduct therapy on him, but to me it was using words in the English language in a more sophisticated way. I was speaking my truth without having to cuss him out or cry to articulate my feelings. I didn't have to get to the angry place to raise an issue with him.

There was a learning curve for him. Sometimes he said, "Nothing's wrong. I'm okay," but I knew that was not the case. I could see it in his body language. I challenged him on it, whereas earlier in our marriage, I would have just let it simmer and simmer inside him.

To this day I'm hypersensitive of people's feelings because of the way I was raised. So when I finally got my voice, I went to the other extreme. If he had a twitch, even if his pupils dilated a certain way, I called him on it.

"What's going on?" I said. "You need to tell me something?"

I'd almost start a fight. His brow would be furrowed, and I knew he was upset about something. He is slow to boil and has a very giving spirit, but when he reaches a certain point, his temper bubbles over. So I started intervening before that happened.

In the beginning he denied anything was going on, but now he's pretty good at acknowledging his feelings.

"Yeah, you did something to upset me," he says.

"Okay. Now we can talk," I respond—because I'm strong enough to handle it.

Anthony

Brigitte did become more outspoken with me. After we'd been married for about twenty years, she called me a [bleep]. I laughed so hard.

"So I've been a [bleep] once in twenty years," I said. "That's a good track record."

Which made her even madder.

Brigitte

Yeah. Five years later I called him a different bleep. But that also made him laugh.

We have an agreement now: He can't work on his gigs in the house, and I can't do therapy on him. It's a demilitarized zone.

Anthony

Brigitte's new profession gave me fresh material:

> My wife is a clinical psychologist. She's always analyzing my
> emotions.
>   "How does that make you feel that I don't cook for you? How
> does it make you feel that I drive a Lexus and you drive a Ford
> Escort?"
>   "Shut up."
>   "Shut up? Oh, guess who's not going to have sex tonight."
>   Women, when a man tells you to shut up, he's already factored
> in that he's not going to have sex tonight.

Brigitte

While I was finding my voice, Anthony started finding his. One time when he
was out on the road, a club owner gave him just one hand towel in his condo
to use for an entire week. What do you do with one hand towel? You wipe
your face and then the rest of your body. What do you do the next day? You
wipe your face with that same little towel that you used everywhere else? My
husband wasn't having *any* of that.

Anthony

I told the club owner, "Look, I'm going to Walmart, I'm getting some towels,
and you're going to reimburse me." That's what I did, and he never invited me
back—because how dare I stand up to him? But I wasn't going to wash my
body with the same hand towel all week.

Another time I was put up at a condo where the door chain was busted,
and there was blood on the couch.

"I can't stay here," I told my fellow comics.

"Where are you going to stay?" they asked.

"I'm going to stay in a hotel."

"But, but . . ."

By then I was the headliner, and I'd been through enough, so I felt more confident in telling the club owner, "You're disrespecting us."

Brigitte

Anthony was finally standing up for himself.

19

Catharsis

I'm a grown man, and I don't know what to do.

Anthony

About ten years after Brittany had passed, before Christmas, I woke up one morning and heard birds chirping outside my window. I loved the sound. It brought me a joy that I hadn't felt in so long. It was as simple as that: I could hear the birds chirping again, and when I went outside, I could smell the roses. Later, when I heard babies laughing, I smiled instead of becoming sad.

For those ten years following our daughter's death, we didn't put up a Christmas tree and pretty much ignored the holiday. Now, for the first time since then, I was hearing Christmas songs on the radio and enjoying them. I wanted to put up decorations.

I was emerging from my cocoon.

Grieving doesn't have a time limit. It doesn't have an expiration date. But I felt like the fog had been lifted, and I could appreciate things again. I don't know why it happened right then. It was just time. Mourning and sorrow had been weighing so heavily on me, but I was moving at last toward that light at the end of the tunnel.

When you come out of a cocoon, you're stronger and have a different purpose than when you went in. A butterfly has the ability to adapt to a new environment. After Brittany's death and everything that followed, including my illness, I became stronger with my faith and developed a deeper understanding that tomorrow is not promised, so you must love and enjoy everyone you're with today. I had a greater appreciation of people. I had a greater appreciation of craft. And as I looked back on my life, I realized that I've always been watched over by God. From living in the projects up to now, I can see that my path has been guided. It wasn't just me mapping it all out on my own.

Knowing that doesn't stop the hurt. If you lose someone close to you, you can't simply say, "Well, it was for a reason." You may or may not believe that, and that's okay. What's confusing on this earth will become clear once we get to the other side. That's when we'll say, "Oh!" Until then we struggle with these questions while trying to keep our faith.

A tragedy pulls some people further away from God because they can't accept a God who would approve of whatever terrible thing had happened. I questioned God for a long time about Brittany but later realized that the ordeal had brought me closer to Him.

When I was younger, I wasn't thinking about death, and no one around me had died. No one teaches you how to act when a loved one, especially a child, passes on. You're almost writing your own book. But as I got older, I became a stronger believer because the Bible became real to me. You read about people going through problems just as you are. When King David lost his son, he said, "Can I bring him back again? I shall go to him, but he shall not return to me" (2 Sam. 12:23). That story now had teeth to me, and I learned from it. As hard as it is now to be without my daughter, I look forward to seeing her and my parents and aunts and uncles again on the other side. I'm here now but not forever. That helps. As the Bible says, there's nothing new under the sun (Eccl. 1:9).

Life is cruel sometimes, and it's okay to have whatever emotion you have when you lose someone you love. I tell people, "Hey, if you want to cry, if you want to get mad, if you want to shout out, God's shoulders are big enough. It's okay. He still has you."

I have one friend who never had children, but when his dog died, it just rocked him. He felt ashamed of talking about it with me because I had lost Brittany, but I told him, "Hey, grief is grief. Loss is loss."

At the suggestion of a woman at our church, I started teaching Sunday school. The kids lived around the Valley and were mostly Hispanic and black.

So while Brigitte was counseling some children, I was teaching the Scriptures to other kids.

None of this was going to bring Brittany back, but it felt right, like it was God's plan for Brigitte and me to give back in other ways.

Soon I felt my daughter's presence even more powerfully.

I was performing at the US Comedy Arts Festival in Aspen, Colorado, in February 2003, when someone from a relatively young nonprofit group called the Moth approached me and a few other comedians about telling a personal story from the stage. The Moth has grown into a huge national storytelling organization, spawning a popular National Public Radio show, *The Moth Radio Hour*, plus a weekly podcast and branches in many US and international cities. But back then it was a small, New York–based organization, founded in 1997 by poet/novelist George Dawes Green and dedicated to promoting unscripted storytelling.

I like telling stories and working without a script. I also appreciated new challenges. So I said okay. I had a couple of days to come up with something. The theme of this program was "When Worlds Collide."

There was no calculation in my thought process. I wasn't aiming to develop a piece that would have legs, something I could perform again and again. This was a one-off, as far as I was concerned. I was at a big comedy festival in Aspen, where you went outside and saw a dog wearing a sweater, and that sweater cost a few thousand dollars. This wasn't a place where you brought out your material about being poor.

With Brigitte home in Los Angeles, I was alone in my hotel room, pondering what story I might tell, and I heard my daughter's voice. Brittany spoke to me in a way she never could in real life.

"Tell my story now," she said.

It was a very emotional moment. Even now I get overwhelmed thinking about it. In the dozen years since Brittany had passed, I had not discussed her onstage or on television or anywhere else in public. Most of my colleagues had no idea I'd even had a daughter. Brigitte and I still kept pictures of her up in our home, and she remained a constant presence for us, but she was ours solely. People on the outside didn't know about her death or, more important, her life.

Now Brittany was calling to me. Although I previously had worried about how her story would reflect on me, how it might change the way people treated or thought about me, this wasn't about me anymore. It was about Brittany. It was about giving my daughter a voice at last.

We weren't supposed to rehearse the Moth pieces a lot, and I had little time to prepare anyway. As I tried to formulate the monologue in my hotel room, I was crying like a baby. Everything was coming back and hitting me hard. I had to find the resolve to tell this story without becoming too emotional because otherwise I'd be whipped. I had to do it for my daughter.

I kept working it out in my head and talking it through in my room. A story like this should sound like it's flowing out of your head, but you must practice and refine it to make it seem that natural.

Stevie Ray Vaughan, the great guitarist-singer-songwriter who died in a helicopter crash at age thirty-five, used to say that you should perform every song like it's either the first time you've played it or the last time you ever will. You must deliver that kind of emotional truth every time you hit the stage. In this case I had no choice. The emotions I conveyed in my Moth monologue were real and raw because this was the first time I'd really explored all the pain that I continued to feel. This, after all these years, was my true therapy.

The day before the performance, the Moth organizer onsite wanted me to give her a quick run-through. With just the two of us in a small room, I started telling the story. Halfway through she was tearing up, and I was too.

"All right, stop," she said. "We've got the beats of where you're going. We'll do it tomorrow."

Some of the other comedians' Moth monologues were powerful. Bill Burr, a stand-up from the Boston area who now hosts the *Monday Morning Podcast*, told a devastating story about how as a six-year-old, after he'd made his mother laugh, his father got mad at him, told him he was giggling and acting like a little girl, and then gave him a doll for Christmas. That crushed him. It took a lot of strength for Bill to tell that story. I gained inspiration from that.

Up to the moment I hit the stage, I was practicing my monologue. Just like the first time I was on *The Tonight Show*, I didn't want to sound stupid.

This program was new for the US Comedy Arts Festival, and far from a big deal. It took place in the late morning, and fewer than twenty people were in the audience when I got up to speak. As I stood there in my tan crew-neck sweater, I was nervous but figured this was it. Everyone who would hear my story was in this small room, and I had no intention of telling it again. It wasn't like I thought, *If this goes well in Aspen, I'll take it on the road*. I didn't know the performance was being filmed and recorded. YouTube didn't yet exist. What we all were about to share was intimate and of the moment, and afterward it would exist solely as a memory.

Although I'd prepared what I was going to say, once the words started flowing, I felt like I was reliving the experience. My delivery was filled with stops and starts because this was so hard and so sad and because I was confronting emotions that I'd kept buried for so long. I wasn't just crafting a piece of storytelling. The story was erupting out of me, with a fury that I hadn't previously revealed or even realized. I used strong language that I never otherwise used. The impact was intense, for me as well as for the audience.

I began on a quiet note:

Charles Dickens's classic tale *A Tale of Two Cities* starts off with the phrase "It was the best of times, it was the worst of times. . . ." In 1990, I moved from Chicago with my family to LA to seek my fame and fortune, and within a couple of weeks of being there, I got two important phone calls. One was from the talent coordinator of *The Tonight Show*, offering me a spot as a comedian on *The Tonight Show*, and the second call was from my daughter's doctor, to say that her cancer had resurfaced. A year prior she was diagnosed with cancer, and we fought it, and it went into remission, and now it was back.

For that next year, my life was pretty surreal. It's like two different personalities. During the day, in order to keep my daughter at home with me, I would have to learn CPR, and how to work a heart monitor, and administer medicine, and all these technical terms, and take her back and forth to get her platelets and blood, and check up on her. And at night I would go from club to club with the talent coordinator, and I would work on my set to try to perfect it. I would meet veterans like George Wallace and Seinfeld and Roseanne, and I thought that everything was great because we had beat the cancer before, we could beat it again, and this was the first time that I was going to be in front of millions of people on *The Tonight Show*.

The first time on *The Tonight Show* I was extremely nervous. All I could think about while I was backstage being introduced was: *Don't mess up. Just don't mess up. Whatever you do, don't mess up.* And the curtains opened, and there's six hundred people and the cameras, and Johnny's over there, and the band is over there, and I don't know what I said for the next six minutes, but I got six applause breaks.

The great part of that night was that I was going to my car, and I met Johnny, who was going to his car, and it was just a private moment between us in the parking lot of him saying, "You were very funny. You were extremely funny. Start working on your second *Tonight Show* because I want you back."

By the time I got the official call for my second *Tonight Show,* my daughter . . .

At this point my voice started to shake. I paused and placed my hands on my hips, reached up and rubbed my nose, and willed myself to continue.

. . . my daughter was admitted to the hospital. If you don't know about cancer, when it comes back, it comes back hard. It's like beating up a gangbanger for the first time, but then he's coming back, and he's coming back meaner and stronger, and he's coming with his friends. So to compensate for that, you have to raise the chemo, and you have to raise the medicine, and you have to raise the radiation, which is difficult for an adult, but she was only two. So she's bald, which she doesn't mind because every kid in the ward is bald, and she thinks it's a part of life. And she can't keep her food down.

By now I couldn't help crying. I could see and hear around me—from the people in the audience to the musician sitting onstage behind me—that I was not the only one.

You're not prepared for this. There's no books. There's no home-ec class to teach you how to deal with this. And you can't go to a therapist because in the black world a therapist is taboo, reserved for rich white people. So you're trying to figure it out. What did I do?

My voice was cracking, tears flowing.

Maybe something I did, maybe something my wife did. Maybe my doctor diagnosed it erroneously. Something.

But at night I still have to be a comic; I still have to work on *The Tonight Show* because that's what I do. I'm a clown. I'm a clown whose medical bills are rising, who's one step away from being evicted, who's one step from getting his car repo'd . . .

My voice was getting higher and louder.

. . . and I have to come out and make you laugh because no one wants to hear the clown in pain because that's not *funny*!

And my humor is becoming dark, and it's biting, and it's becoming hateful, and the talent coordinator is seeing that there's a problem because NBC is all about nice, and everything is going to be okay, and we're starting to buck horns because he wants everything light, and I want to be honest and tell life, and I'm hurting, and I want everybody else to hurt! Because somebody is to blame for this!

So I buck up, and I suppress my anger, and I form and develop a nice, cute routine for the second *Tonight Show*. And I get applause breaks. And I get asked to come back for a third time.

And I'm perfecting my third set, and the doctor asks me to come in, and I know something's wrong because even the doctor is crying, and doctors don't cry. And he said, "We've done all we can. There's nothing else for us to do."

I said, "How much time does she have?"

And he said, "At the most, at the most . . . six weeks." And I should plan for that.

And I'm thinking, *How do I plan for that? I haven't planned to buy her her first bicycle. I haven't planned to walk her to school.*

I was crying by now, my voice pitching higher.

I haven't planned to take pictures of her on her prom. I haven't planned to walk her down the aisle to get married. How am I going to plan to buy her a dress to be buried in?

And I'm trying to keep it together because I'm the man, and I'm the man of the house, and I don't want to cry, but it's coming. And I'm trying to tell my wife, tell myself, Tony, I'm trying to beg the world: "Just give me a chance. Just give me a chance. Just let me take a breath. Just stop this for a minute."

I want to call my parents and ask them, "What do I do?"

I don't know what to do. I'm a grown man, and I don't know what to do.

And a voice in me comes up like Denzel [Washington] from *Training Day: MAN UP, N*****! You think you the only one losing kids today? Twenty-five kids walked in here with cancer! Only five walking out! This ain't no sitcom! It don't wrap up all nice and tidy in thirty minutes! This is life! Welcome to the real world!*

And he was right. So I bucked up because that's what I'm supposed to do. And on my third *Tonight Show*, by that time my daughter had died. And I had six applause breaks that night. No one knew I was mourning. No one knew that I couldn't care less about *The Tonight Show* or Johnny Carson.

In 1990[-91] I had three appearances with the legendary Johnny Carson and a total of fourteen applause breaks, and I would have given it all if I could just have one more day sharing a bag of french fries with my daughter.

It was the best of times. It was the worst of times. Thank you.

I was weeping. The audience was in tears. I thought, *Hmmm. This doesn't really feel like a comedy festival. Did I go too far?*

After the show people were coming up to me saying, "I lost someone," "I lost a friend," "I lost a loved one," "I lost my grown child." And "Thank you."

When I shouted the *N*-word, that's something I never would have said on my own. But I was quoting Denzel, and it was true to the moment.

The Moth invited me to perform the monologue again in New York, where the organization is based, and in Washington, DC, where it was presenting a show. Those performances went fine. My delivery was smoother.

And that was it. I'd told Brittany's story, and it was cathartic. I felt like I'd removed a heavy weight from my shoulders. Now I could return to doing my work and living my life.

Brigitte

I didn't listen to Anthony's Moth monologue until years later. By then all of my friends had seen it on YouTube. One really good friend, Lisa, used to ask me, "Are you ready to see it yet?"

"If I do," I said, "it won't be with an audience of people looking at me."

I dreaded watching it, but finally, one day I snuck a look at it. You know what? I was proud of him. I was really proud of him because it was organic. He had let go of all of those inhibitions about Hollywood and how he was perceived. He no longer was worried that if he revealed the truth about himself, no one would pick up the phone and call him for work anymore. That was the first time I saw that he didn't care.

Then I started reading the comments on YouTube about how inspired people were, but after a while I had to stop. It was too much.

This was a lot for me to take in, but at the same time it was his journey, so I was somewhat removed from it. I allowed myself to hear him and to see him, and I knew him well enough to know that he had really, really exposed himself on that stage.

And when he used the *N*-word, I was like, "Oh! What!? Ahhh, he is not *playing* with you all." I was very, very proud of him for what he was sharing with his audience—and with me. I saw for the first time what Brittany's death was like for him.

After he did the Moth, Anthony became more transparent about his life—except for one area that he kept hidden. I suggested that now that he had told Brittany's story, he might want to let people know about his MS so they would understand what actually was happening with him and maybe even could help.

That still took a while.

20

The Last Reveal

I got hit by a car in Detroit, so I was able to make a little extra money on the side. As soon as I got hit, I started rolling on the ground, holding my head: "I can't see. Is my Lexus okay?"

The guy who hit me looked down. "You ain't got no Lexus."

I looked up. "I do now."

Anthony

By the time I did the Moth, my mom had been diagnosed with lung cancer even though she had never been a smoker. At that time she was living alone in a condo in Chicago's West Loop. My stepfather, Fred Johnson, died in 1998 of a ruptured aorta while he was working as a doorman in Presidential Towers, one of the West Loop's first upscale residential high-rises. He and my mom had an apartment there in addition to their house on the South Side.

I never grew close to my stepfather. In marrying my mother, he didn't view being an active father to my brother and me as part of the deal. We didn't bond, and he remained a distant figure throughout my life. When we sat across the breakfast table from each other, he preferred to read the cereal box than to talk to me or Danny. He never asked, "What are you planning to do today?" He didn't shoot the breeze. I never played catch with him. I never did anything with him.

I do remember, though, that Brittany could pull his hair and climb all over him, and he never complained. I was glad I got to see that side of him.

Most important, he loved my mother. I loved my stepfather because he loved my mom. We all loved Mom. He would do everything he could for her. Their relationship was golden.

Brigitte

After her husband passed away, Anthony's mother didn't want to be at Presidential Towers anymore, so she purchased a condo on Canal Street by the Chicago River. She was a very healthy, active woman. She didn't drink or smoke.

After she was diagnosed with cancer, she didn't want the grandkids—Anthony's brother's children—to know. When they came over, she put on her wig and had her eyebrows painted on. She was ill for less than a year and a half. She got everything in order. She was prepared for death.

Anthony

My mom became very skinny. The doctors at the hospital finally told us, "There's no more we can do for her." Hospitals generally don't keep patients whom they no longer can treat, so we found a nice assisted-living place for her in Chicago's Gold Coast. She was only sixty.

Her body was telling her it was time to exit, and eventually she stopped eating. The doctor asked my brother and me whether they should give her a feeding tube, but we knew that's not what she would have wanted, and the doctor said it might cause more complications than it was worth. My mom already had told us she didn't want to be resuscitated or to have extreme measures taken to extend her life. She also gave us instructions for once she was gone: "Have a funeral, but after the burial don't visit the grave because that's not where I'll be."

I was in tears as she said this, but I appreciated knowing she was ready for her transition.

I was especially close to her because I was the firstborn. I was the responsible one. If she gave me something to do, I did it. If she gave me a dollar in the store, I would find something to buy for her. In a way she was training me for Mother's Day and her birthday, both of which she cared about, in part because she worked so hard for us the rest of the year.

"Please acknowledge me on Mother's Day," she said. "Please acknowledge me on my birthday. I washed your dirty drawers, so at least acknowledge me on the important days of my life."

My stepfather couldn't have cared less about these holidays. But I always remembered.

I had no regrets when she died, like I should've done this or that. I did right by her. I was good. I loved her and showed it, and she knew.

In some ways Brittany's death prepared me for my mom's, yet in some ways I took this one even harder. With Brittany I'd known my role and was able to stick with it: the father and warrior fighting the good fight. When my mom passed, I literally could not talk for a week or two. I learned what dying of a broken heart felt like because for the first time, I had to live without the person who had been supporting me from the moment I began to breathe. This is true for a lot of boys, but especially black boys from single-parent households where the mom had to be the mom *and* the dad. No matter how tough or hard we think we are, we're rocked when we lose our mothers. They're our everything.

My mom had been my biggest cheerleader. To become a comic or an escape artist, to get to Hollywood—she never said I couldn't do any of those things. Sometimes she said, "I don't know *how* you're going to do it," but she always had faith that I could. The sky was the limit with my mom when it came to her dreams for me. Brigitte has since filled that void to the tenth power: "You can do it, honey, and don't believe those who say you can't." She gets militant about it. But my mom, for me, had been like oxygen.

My mother followed Brittany and my stepfather to a resting place at Washington Memorial Cemetery. The three of them were together, and we felt our loss. I also knew we'd be reunited someday.

In the meantime, I continued on with my life and career, though doing so was becoming more difficult.

Brigitte

Anthony wouldn't say anything about his MS. He was in the closet about it for years, just as he had been about Brittany. He didn't want anyone to know, not even our friends.

That was tough because I was trying to help him, and I felt like I was doing it all by myself. We were running on fumes as his condition worsened. I finally confided in Ron Pearson, a comedian friend of Anthony's.

"Anthony's got a neurological issue, and I can't do this by myself, Ron. I really, really need your support, but Anthony feels very uncomfortable with coming out about this."

"Brigitte, you have my support," he said. "We won't violate Anthony's privacy. We'll wait till he discusses it."

By this time Anthony was slurring his words, his speech had slowed down, he was walking unsteadily, and he had developed more balance and dexterity issues. Because his voice had started to go, it had a quavering quality—you can hear it in the Moth monologue, though most people chalked that up to how emotional he was. Outside of that context, his vocal shakiness was interpreted differently.

"Are you nervous?" a director would ask at an audition.

"No," he'd say—and offer no more explanation.

When he wouldn't get the part, his agent or manager would report that the casting director had said, "Anthony seemed nervous."

Some openly wondered whether Anthony was drinking or using drugs. That became the Hollywood scuttlebutt, even though he was the last person who would have had either of those problems. People were observing Anthony's struggles but didn't know the how or why, so they were reaching their own conclusions.

Ron told me that a director on a project approached him to ask, "Is Anthony okay?"

"Yeah, he's fine; he's good," Ron said.

I spoke with Anthony about this and tried to get him to clear the air.

"Honey, I know LA is superficial," I said, "but we really, really have to think about what's going to happen when you go to this audition. You need to teach people how to treat you because if someone is trying to figure out something that they don't have a scenario for, they will fill in the blanks."

But he wouldn't discuss it. For years he wasn't ready.

Anthony

My manager and agent still didn't know about my MS—because I wouldn't tell them. I concealed it for a long time, even though Brigitte kept telling me, "If you don't tell people, they'll assume the worst." She felt it would behoove me to write my narrative instead of letting others think up their own stories. But I refused.

It wasn't until after I did the Moth that I had the courage to address the MS. I was feeling more confident about speaking my truth.

Yet that monologue was about Brittany. I did the Moth for her. This was about me, which in some ways made it harder to talk about.

I didn't have a publicist issue any sort of announcement. Facebook and Twitter weren't yet around to serve as a vehicle for sharing such information. I was my usual low-key self and told some friends first.

Some were crushed and started crying. Because they knew so little about MS, they interpreted the news as if I were already dead. I saw them tearing up, breaking down, and I thought, *This person can't be in my life right now because I don't need that energy around me while I'm trying to navigate this journey.*

Others were more constructive.

"This makes sense," some of my friends said. "When you told us you wouldn't be playing basketball anymore, that seemed strange, but now we get it."

Some were inquisitive: "What do you need from us? Is there anything we can do?" I tried to teach them what I knew about my condition, and I offered suggestions on how they might help.

I especially appreciated the comics because they were funny.

"Oh," they said, "we just thought you were getting old."

Brigitte

Some men told him, "Dude, I don't know what to say." Those were the ones I admired the most, the ones who acknowledged their vulnerability and admitted, "I don't know what to say."

Good. Don't say anything. Just be. It's cool. It's good. Just don't abandon him. Please don't abandon him.

Anthony

This whole experience, while challenging, reinforced the bond between Brigitte and me. She's a great teammate and always has my back.

I appreciated that she didn't pull the trigger in telling people about my condition until I decided to go public. When I didn't want to tell anyone, she said, "Okay, we won't tell anybody." When I didn't want to take a certain medication, she said, "Okay." And when I finally said I'd go public and take the medicine, she was ready to go. She respected my decisions since it was my journey first and foremost.

Over the course of our marriage, I went from thinking *Me, me, me* to *We, we, we.* It took me a while to realize that everything I did involved her.

Early in our marriage, when she said, "Call me to let me know if you're going to be out late," I thought she was trying to control me.

Guys on the street said, "You're whupped."

"No," she told me, "I just want to know if you're dead."

Over time I appreciated that she wasn't trying to pry. She was thinking of my best interests. She was the ideal helpmate for me—and she's much smarter than I am.

Now that I was revealing all that I had kept hidden, I felt like a giant burden had been lifted. Hollywood is a land of make-believe, but I no longer was pretending. My story was my story, and I was living it out in the open for the first time since I had arrived in Los Angeles so many years earlier.

That's not to say that my newfound transparency worked wonders for my career. Once I told people in the industry about my condition, I naively thought, *Now they'll be sympathetic and give me roles.* That hasn't been the case. The people in the entertainment business may have empathy, but that doesn't mean they want to hire a comedian/actor displaying MS symptoms. On TV and in film you don't see a lot of people with disabilities getting cast. To the casting people I brought up Michael J. Fox, who has Parkinson's disease but still does some acting work.

"Yeah," they said, "but that's Michael J. Fox."

Brigitte

Anthony was just as good of an actor, dramatic actor, as he was a comic, but when his disease started to come to the fore, those talents became less visible. I still feel that there's an audience for him. I think his vision was just postponed to some extent. When you find yourself with a disability, you must redefine how you share your gift with the world. You must look at it differently, but your goals and objectives can remain the same. For Anthony that transformation took place on the stage.

The older he got, the more he started to share his experiences with his audience. One thing about Anthony is he could always make the drab seem really, really funny because he doesn't like people feeling sorry for him. I appreciated that about him. I knew when he started disclosing bits and pieces of his illness that he was on his way to being seen more seriously.

Anthony

The first time I went blind, I was driving on the freeway to a play rehearsal. Everything started to get dark, so I assumed a major rainstorm was coming. I turned on the windshield wipers, but that didn't help.

It got darker and darker, and it occurred to me that my sight might be going. I thought I'd better get off the freeway, so I did the stupid thing and put on my blinkers, which caused everyone to speed up to prevent me from changing lanes. Eventually I was able to exit, and I looked for a parking place. My eyesight was down to about 50 percent. I couldn't find a spot and circled around as the light kept dimming. Finally, I found a place to pull over, my sight now at about 20 percent.

I got out of my car and stood there for a while. I'm six feet four and black, so nobody was going to bother me. My other senses kicked in. I could hear women walking, which sounded different from guys walking. I could smell pizza and cologne. I was able to see just enough to get across the street so I could call Brigitte.

Brigitte

Anthony was standing in the middle of the sidewalk, looking so disoriented and lost and afraid. People were just passing him by. When I got to him, he was upset, understandably so. I took him to the emergency room in Burbank.

Anthony

When we got to the ER, the emergency room workers handed me a form and told me, "Fill this out."

"I can't because I'm *blind*," I said.

"You can't see this eye chart?"

"No."

By then it was night. After waiting three or four hours in the emergency room, I grew frustrated and said, "Let's go. I'll talk to my neurologist in the morning." When I did, I told him I thought the blindness was related to the MS, but he said, "It's not the MS. MS doesn't do this."

My eyesight returned after one day. Later I told the people in my MS support group, "I went blind last week. Has that happened to anyone?"

Everyone's hands went up. Yes, that is one of the symptoms. This was when I realized I knew as much as the experts, and I began to read more about MS. There's no cure for it, but it affects everyone differently. I can stand and talk for a long time, whereas other people with MS are in wheelchairs. Talk-show host Montel Williams has discussed how his feet are very tender and he has pain every day because of his MS. Something I always remember is that someone is always worse off than you.

I was in relatively good shape when I took part in a faith-based comedy tour that turned into a movie and DVD. The Apostles of Comedy was designed as a sort of family-friendly version of the very popular Blue Collar Comedy Tour, which starred Jeff Foxworthy, Bill Engvall, Ron White, and Larry the Cable Guy from 2000 to 2006. The Apostles of Comedy had some of the same producers and featured me and three other "clean" Christian comics: Jeff Allen (who's also from Chicago), Brad Stine, and Ron Pearson, a good friend whose daughter is my goddaughter.

"Get ready for laughter of a higher power," went the tagline for the movie, which came out in 2008. We filmed two performances in Nashville, and the movie intercut our routines with clips of us talking with each other about comedy and life. I didn't change up my set for this audience, though they especially appreciated my riffs on being raised Baptist.

I was in church all day on Sunday. I wanted to be a Catholic so bad when I was growing up. I used to envy Catholics. Catholics, they got in and out. One hour means one hour to a Catholic. I've seen Catholics riot after one hour. "Hey! [pointing to wristwatch] Hey! . . . We gonna be late for bingo."

I would have Catholic friends come over: "Hey, man, play some football?"

"I got to go to church."

"We'll play when you get out."

"Uh-uh. I'm Baptist. You won't see me until Monday." Because we would stay in church: sunrise service, Sunday school, regular service, and then we go visit the sister church, come back for evening service. People wonder why we see visions? We hungry. After the third service I'm walking around, "I see a chicken sandwich. . . ."

I also reflected back on my childhood.

I grew up in the inner city on two things: church and Pepto-Bismol. My mother gave me Pepto-Bismol for everything. No matter what ailed me, Pepto-Bismol. Do you know how much Pepto-Bismol you have to take to recover from a gunshot?

And when I wanted to talk about kids, I invoked relatives.

Teenagers are not human. I'm trying to raise my seventeen-year-old cousin, he's six seven, and he swears he's God's gift to mankind. He's always lifting weights at night, like he's in lockdown. Always trying to gauge how strong I am.

"Hey, man, how much can you bench press?"

"I don't know."

"Well, how many push-ups can you do?"

"I don't know."

"You wanna wrestle?"

"No."

"Why? You scared? You scared of these guns?"

"If I was scared of you, I'd choke you in your sleep."

I also talked about my grandmother, who was still around. Speaking in my best approximation of her voice, I said:

"You still gotta protect yourself. Like my late husband always said . . . um . . . what'd he always say? Well, whatever it was, he always said it. I miss him. We did everything together. We was married for, uh, let's see. . . . Lincoln freed the slaves in 1864, Uncle Cephas met his second cousin in 1912, Chubby Checker came out with 'The Twist' in '60—we was married for two years."

That's the only way my grandmother can remember anything. She always has to start with the emancipation of the slaves.

"Grandma, you need anything at the grocery store?"

"Do I need anything? Do I need anything? Um, uh, lemme see . . . [muttering] Lincoln freed the slaves 1864, Chubby Checker came out with 'The Twist,' I went to the grocery store on Wednesday—no, I'm good."

The shows went over great, but the tour didn't really take off. Clean Christian comedy was seen as a novelty, and we performed in churches, which made marketing to the mainstream difficult. As comics, we'd all come out of the nightclubs, but people still thought, *Comedy in church? That doesn't sound like fun.*

You can still buy the DVD, and it includes some revealing exchanges. At one point I sum up how I now view my professional mission:

I believe I can touch people through hardships that I've had. As a comic, I'm just here to make you laugh.

The most emotional moment comes when all four of us are chatting on café couches, and Ron Pearson asks, "Did anything that happened with your daughter affect how you told jokes or what you felt your job was as a comedian? And how did you get out of that spiritually, that place?"

Well, when my daughter died, I was not angry. I was confused. I wanted to know, I wanted to ask God—because I was the perfect father, so when she passed, I was just confused. . . . Like most people, my first response was, "When I get to heaven, that's going to be the first question: 'Why?'"

You go through the stages of loss. You have anger, depression, and you can work on depression. You can be depressed for, I think, a good ten years . . . and still function, still make people laugh, still go through life. But it wasn't until maybe ten years later that I started hearing the birds chirp again, smelling the roses. So in that process of searching, God began to reveal to me. . . .

Because like a lawyer, you never ask a question if you don't know the answer. . . . What if [God] said, "It's because of something you did in your past"?

I didn't want to hear that.

What if God said, "She was supposed to die at [age] three. I didn't want to tell you"?

I didn't want to hear that because I couldn't enjoy the three years of life with her. So, in God's wisdom, the peace that I have is that He said that she's in a better place, she's with her [fighting back tears] . . . she's with her grandparents, and I will see her again. And I understood that.

So I just make people laugh. That's my ministry. . . . I meet people individually, and they say, "Hey, this has happened, this has happened, this has happened."

I was diagnosed with MS fourteen years ago. The death of my daughter, the death of my parents, equipped me for MS.

I go, "Okay," because I look at life as if it's a great novel that you read, and . . . it's a page-turner, and the star of that book is you. And you turn the next page, and the main character loses his daughter, but it's so compelling you keep going.

"Don't you just want to close the book for a while?" Ron asks.

No, because it's so thrilling because this book is making you cry, laugh, get mad, get angry. You keep going, you keep going because you want to see: What's the end?

Now, the author of the book is God. And this is the thing: You already know there's a sequel. That's the peace I have. So every day I go, *I wonder what God has in store for me?*

21

Ties Bound Tight

I just got back from Alaska. They have there what's called the Black Bear Excursion in a remote part of the state. Now, there's not a lot of things that I believe separate blacks from whites—except for maybe Black Bear Excursions. Because I don't know any brother I could call up and say, "Check this out. I got two free tickets for us to go look for some black bears in a remote part of the state."

Anthony

I'm onstage at the Comedy & Magic Club. It takes me longer to get up there than it used to, and people notice that I'm using a white, red-rimmed cane, which I prop against the back wall before I step to the microphone. I'm not trying to hide it. I'm working it into my comedy as I keep doing what I do: telling stories and making people laugh.

I'm going blind, which is why I have my cane. In the hood you can't play Marco Polo because no one will say anything. I go, "Marco . . . Marco . . . Come on. I smell the weed. I know you're here."

Over the years my eyesight has worsened, and it has reached the point where I'm legally blind. I can see where I'm going during the day, but my night vision stinks. I walk with a white cane to let others know about my blindness; it's actually illegal to carry a white cane unless your vision is impaired. I take classes at the Braille Institute, including a cooking class that I love.

My dexterity is not what it was either. What the MS has forced me to do is to rely on people to stay independent. This has been a good thing. When I first was diagnosed, I tried to hide it, and people knew something was going on but didn't know what. Now I lead with, "Hey, could you do this for me? Could you handle this?"

"Sure, no problem."

Many people know someone with MS or lupus or some other disease, and they understand. I'm reminded of how lucky I am to be living at the time of the Americans with Disabilities Act. There are more avenues for assistance than ever before.

For too long I avoided discussing the challenges of my life in my work. Now I realize that speaking my truth, no matter how painful or difficult, is an essential part of creating art. I'm lucky to be in a field where I get to talk about what I'm experiencing.

I've come a long way to get back onto this stage. Before I refocused on my career, Brigitte and I spent three years living in the mountains.

In 2008, someone in the government flagged Brigitte's résumé and recruited her to train as a forensic psychologist, so we drove about two hours north to Tehachapi, California, a small mountain town at an elevation of 4,000 feet, for her interview. They hired and accepted her into the government program, and soon we were living among the wildlife while Brigitte spent every day inside Tehachapi State Prison (aka the California Correctional Institution), a maximum-security facility, analyzing high-profile criminals.

After spending so much time focusing on my career, we were following her lead. I was happy about that. She grew her wings in a job that allowed her to use all of her intelligence and inquisitiveness.

Brigitte

I loved it. Even though I was in a forensic environment, it was one of the safest situations I'd been in. If you tell black people you're going up to Tehachapi, they assume you're visiting someone in prison. More white people associate the place with beautiful golf courses, wineries, and the forest. There were also a post office, a church, a gas station, and a farmers' market.

We had friends up there and lived in a gated community called Bear Valley Springs, which was surrounded by a forest preserve and golf course. We lived near the ninth hole. It was an animal-protected area. The animals did not have to comply with our needs; we had to comply with theirs. We turned off the patio lights to watch the deer cross the street. There were bears—though I rarely saw them—elk that seemed to stand ten feet tall, mountain lions, and sheep. The sheepherders always looked dusty.

Anthony

We saw deer, rabbits, coyotes, and eagles from our home in Bear Valley Springs. I saw an owl swoop down and grab a cat. That owl was huge. That cat was not protected.

Tehachapi was like Mayberry from *The Andy* [not Anthony] *Griffith Show*. There was one movie theater. The tallest building was a Kmart. It was a slower way of living. Unlike Los Angeles, this town experienced all four seasons.

The community was quiet and filled with people either training to be forensic psychologists or to assume other government positions. All of our neighbors were involved with government in some capacity. When I told people that I was a comic, they reacted, "Yeah, right. Okay. That's your cover? That's what you're going to say?"

I had to silence the voice in my head that asked, "So what do *I* do?" The nearest airport was hours away, so scheduling out-of-town gigs was difficult, though I did drive back to LA for acting classes. Otherwise, I learned to relax and enjoy our time in the mountains.

Brigitte

It was one of the best times of my life as well as one of the most strenuous because of the work. What they called training was trial by fire.

I worked in an area of the prison called Special Needs. These were high-profile inmates, and when they were sentenced to prison terms, we assessed their fitness and states of mind.

We constantly had to be on guard because these inmates would try to profile us to find some advantage. If I wasn't sharp enough, they would find my weaknesses and exploit them. I couldn't bring a cell phone, pen, or pencil into the facility because a prisoner might use it against me. We learned about all of the objects that could be made into shanks. One ex-CIA agent who worked there was coaxed into slipping paper and pencils and then stamps to some inmates and even mailing their letters, which was forbidden. He had to be walked off the yard.

One inmate once told me, "Doc, you look like you drive a fancy car." I could have written him up for engaging with me like that, but I did have a fancy car at the time—I drove a beautiful new royal blue Lexus—so I played along.

"Really? What kind of car do you fantasize me driving?"

"I see you driving a Lexus."

"What? What color?"

"A light color."

At least he got the last part wrong.

"She looks like she's from the Midwest," I heard another inmate say about me. "She don't take no [bleep]."

I was freaked out a few times. One guy slit his wrists vertically right in front of me, and I saw other instances of disturbing or threatening behavior. But I kept my cool. If someone was shouting or doing something inappropriate as I passed by his cell, I didn't break stride. And when I was meeting with the inmates, armed guards protected me, as did the stab vest I had to wear.

One agent told me, "You must have had a messed-up childhood."

"Why?"

"You don't flinch."

Anthony

Brigitte wasn't scared. She had grown up with her mother.

Brigitte

The time passed so quickly. Every time I went through the gate, I thought, *I am so blessed that I can walk out of here in seven and a half hours.*

Eventually we had to return to our former life. Anthony's illness had progressed, the specialists were not in the mountains, and taking him down to LA for appointments and treatments proved too strenuous. So we moved to the Valley at the end of 2011, me with my training and forensics license and Anthony with more stories and jokes to tell.

Anthony

> I used to live in Tehachapi. . . . There are not a lot of brothers up there. Even the coyotes were going, "Uh . . ." A coyote came up to me, and he didn't know whether he should eat me or pee on me. It's funny because I was thinking the same thing. We just dapped.

For these Comedy & Magic Club shows, I performed on consecutive Friday and Saturday nights, when the club typically features ten comics without revealing the lineup to customers. The hallway walls are lined with photos of comedians who have played this iconic place over the years, including Jay Leno, Robin Williams, Jerry Seinfeld, Arsenio Hall, and, yes, me.

Before one Saturday's show, Arsenio and I see each other in the hallway and exchange hugs and pose for photos together. Robert Wuhl, of HBO's *Arli$$* and the first Tim Burton *Batman* movie, was on the bill, too, plus New York comedian Steven Scott, a comic magician named Joel Ward (someone had to bring the magic to the Comedy & Magic Club), and a pair of veteran comics with whom I've been friendly over the years: Bobby Collins and Jack Coen, the latter a longtime writer-producer for *The Tonight Show with Jay Leno*. As we await our sets, we catch up on each other's lives and careers in the greenroom, which hasn't changed much after all these years. The cinder-block walls still boast the signatures, wisecracks, and drawings of so many of the comedians who have appeared here, and an old tube television set near the door shows whichever performer is onstage. As you sit at the long table that stretches alongside the mirrored wall, you can order dinner, which owner Mike Lacey still provides for the comics and their guests.

When it's time to go on, I slip out of the greenroom and step through another doorway to the back of the small stage. I'm following Arsenio, who has been whipping everyone up with a booming, fist-pumping, profanity-filled set aimed largely at the White House's current occupant. (Arsenio is a former *Celebrity Apprentice* winner.) When I take the stage after him, the dynamic is the opposite of when I used to open for Bernie Mac. My quiet delivery comes across almost as a deadpan after Arsenio's boisterous performance. Now that he has knocked everyone back in their seats, they lean in for me.

> I met a guy, and he went to the Running of the Bulls in Spain. I said, "Why?" and he said, "It's fun. You get drunk, and you wait for them to release the bulls, and then you run for your life."
>
> You know, I grew up in the inner city, and on many occasions I had to run for my life.
>
> It was never fun.

Much of the audience was young enough to be my kids, but they were laughing hard. I was in my element. If I hadn't been able to keep doing stand-up, I might have stopped working in the industry. I've lived through the five stages of a Hollywood career:

Who is Anthony Griffith?
I like Anthony Griffith.
I want Anthony Griffith.
I want someone like Anthony Griffith.
Who is Anthony Griffith?

I'm not actively chasing auditions anymore but still take the occasional movie or TV part. I grew a beard to play the old man of Nyashi Hatendi's 2018 short *Moving On*, and I have an agent who specifically works with handicapped performers and helps keep me active.

It has become harder to sustain a career solely on the club circuit. The pay has changed little over the past couple of decades, and I'm now older than the typical clubgoer and performer. Once you're in your forties or, now, fifties, the young kids going to the comedy clubs can't relate to you as much. They may think you're funny, but they won't connect like they would to a comic in his or her twenties or early thirties.

At the same time the skills for doing stand-up don't go away, nor does the enjoyment. The veterans who live long enough become legends. Don Rickles was ninety and still doing stand-up when he died. Joan Rivers was active up till she passed away at eighty-one. You don't lose your abilities or talent as you get older. You just learn more stories along the way. Jay Leno still has his craft, and people enjoy him whether he's on television, at a corporate event, or headlining a Sunday night at the Comedy & Magic Club. Fame propels you to a certain point, but your skill sustains you.

When I performed at a Comedy & Magic Club anniversary celebration, the young comics and veterans fed off each other's energy. I empathized with what the young performers were going through as they tried to make names for themselves while learning their craft. Some of them will break through and become stars. Some will not. I appreciated that I could step aside and observe the process.

These young comics also inspired me. There was a Jewish guy whose parents converted to Islam, and he was so funny. Another guy, he was playing football, he's Hindu, and said he got hit so hard that he saw Jesus. He said you've got to be hit really hard to see someone else's religion. That made me laugh and made me want to keep finding new and funny things to talk about. I still love being among creative people. One of the young comics regarded me as an OG—"original gangster," legend—and paid me homage: "This is a guy who's been there."

I liked that. It beat saying, "This dude is old."

Aside from stand-up I've had other professional avenues open up for me—corresponding, not coincidentally, with when I started opening up *about* me.

When I delivered that Moth monologue in Aspen back in 2003, I had no idea that anyone would ever see or hear it again. Back then, *viral* was a word you associated with illness, and sharing was something that didn't involve clicking.

As of mid-2018, the YouTube clip of "The Moth Presents Anthony Griffith: The Best of Times, The Worst of Times" had been viewed more than two million times, and more people had listened to it on *The Moth Radio Hour* and *The Moth Podcast*. I had performed in so many movies and TV episodes where my work was either not seen or had minimal impact, yet when I delivered a nine-minute monologue in a small room—without even knowing it was being recorded—it was as if I'd written and starred in a hit show.

It was several years after performing it that my tribute to Brittany went on the Internet. I knew something was up because I was blogging at the time, and all of a sudden my comments board filled up with people telling me how moved they were by my Moth piece, how they'd also lost someone special, how they'd taken solace and inspiration from my words. I was shocked that it had reached so many people and that so many were trying to connect with me. I have tunnel vision about my work—always thinking about the next thing I have to do— so I had no idea of the clip's magnitude, but when I saw it had reached more than a million views, I thought, *Oh!*

Guys got rocked the hardest. They told me they were listening in the car and had to pull over because they were thinking, *Oh, man, if something happened to my kid, would I be able to go on?* They said they hugged their kids a little longer and harder when they put them to bed. I think women are stronger than we are; they mourn differently but have to keep going because they're moms. Guys, when we get knocked down, we get knocked down— though mothers also told me they hugged their kids longer.

So many people reached out to me, and I responded to every one of them.

Brigitte

Kids wrote to Anthony and said they delivered his monologue in school because it was one of their favorites. Students in acting classes asked permission to perform it. Some dancers created modern performance pieces around his words. Anthony's monologue took on so many new lives. He wasn't getting paid for any of this, but people showed respect and asked permission.

Anthony

"Sure. Why not?" I always said.

When I watched young actors delivering my monologue, I critiqued the performances to myself: *No, you should do it like this.* But I appreciated that they were seeking my blessing and creating new art.

I get asked to do more speaking engagements now. I appear a lot at churches and corporate and charity events, whether doing stand-up or giving speeches or some combination. People want to hear me talk about my life, with or without jokes. I've been discussing my MS as well as what happened with Brittany, and a lot of people afterward tell me about their battles with lupus or other autoimmune diseases.

As one of the informal ambassadors for the National Multiple Sclerosis Society, I emcee events and try to raise awareness when I can. My mantra is that you can have a very fulfilling life in spite of the disability. I was never a "woe is me" type person. I've never sought pity. I follow the example of my mom, who I thought could do anything no matter the circumstance. Tough times should not stop you from doing all you can do or being all you can be. It's still on you to fulfill your dreams or destiny. The challenges, no matter how big or small, give you character.

I was in Austin, Texas, recently to perform at a fund-raiser to help kids whose parents are incarcerated. The organizers wanted comedy but also asked me to stick to the evening's theme. So I talked about when my mom bought me a straitjacket for Christmas and related it to the Bible story in which the king says, "When I was hungry, you fed me. When I was thirsty, you gave me a drink. When I was a stranger, you took me in. When I was naked, you clothed me" (Matt. 25:35–36, paraphrased).

"When did we do this, King?" the people ask him.

"Whatever you did for one of the least of these brothers and sisters of mine, you did for me," the king replies (v. 40 NIV).

That was the through line of my story, that the smallest acts of kindness may be the ones that have the most lasting impact. When my mom bought me a straitjacket, that was my best Christmas. She made me so happy. She exceeded her expected duties.

"Go beyond your comfort level," I tell people, "and you will make your kids happy, and they will remember that for the rest of their lives."

I'm working on a one-man show because, here's the thing, there are more baby boomers than millennials. And the cool part about being in my fifties is there's a whole audience out there who can relate to my experiences. With baby boomers you can be funny, tell stories, and talk about life. Creating a one-man show will help extend the shelf life of what I do.

Brigitte

After returning from the mountains, I continued to work with the state as a forensic psychologist, but now I'm exclusively doing clinical work. Over time

I have gravitated toward working with children younger than twelve months old who communicate in nonverbal ways, with a language of their own.

"How do you do therapy with an infant?" many people ask.

The genesis of that stems from my doctoral work that studied children with leukemia who are preverbal. I've always been humbled by a child's ability to communicate his or her needs without uttering words. With Brittany I had to translate what she was trying to tell me via her intonations or the frequency of her cries—if she wanted a diaper change or was in pain or was hungry. We had to learn new ways to communicate to make sure her needs were being met.

Aside from being inspired by my daughter, my interest was driven by my own childhood issues. In order to communicate with these very young children, I must communicate with the caregivers. I work with mothers who experience postpartum depression or maybe even psychosis, and I help them learn to serve their children's needs. I assist the mother in appreciating what certain glances and utterances really mean. Some of this work springs from wishful thinking on my part. I hark back to my childhood and feel regret that my mom didn't do any of this with me.

Sometimes I still get triggered. I can tell when a baby is in pain. Those pain cries can get to you as a parent; I feel so sorry for the kids. I have a private practice, with an office in Sherman Oaks, and I work with parents and children of all ages, often in families connected to the entertainment industry. With my concierge service, I travel to studios, offices, and homes to do consultations as well.

I give back to the community as a contractor with the California Department of Disability Services, working with clients in Lancaster—a city about sixty miles north of Los Angeles—where I serve a diverse population who never would be exposed to therapy otherwise. I assess children for disabilities, and through that work I have become a specialist in autism. I see kids who are under three, and they're absolutely adorable, and the state reimburses me so the parents don't have to pay. I treat these young patients as if they were my private practice clients. I roll out the red carpet for them.

I'm enriched by being around children and helping them or just enjoying their presence. When I hear or see a happy baby now, that makes me happy. I don't feel that negative pang.

I couldn't do this work if Brittany hadn't bestowed her legacy and gift to me. She's the reason I'm able to help so many people and get such fulfillment doing so. At the same time, I know that I'm working out my fantasy of what my own childhood might have been like if my mother had been a different, more understanding person.

"Honey, you're advocating for the small Bridge," Anthony said to me, making the connection and giving me a verbal hug. "This is how you're taking care of the Bridge who didn't have that, through your work, through other children. This is how you're taking care of the little you."

"Oh, you understand!"

Anthony

I was teaching vacation Bible school, and there was one girl who was so cute. She was dark, very dark, and I thought, *Wow. She's like Brittany might have been.*

That I'm able to help children like Brittany fuels me. I've gotten to teach and to know so many kids over more than twenty years of teaching Sunday school. You don't realize how old you are until you see a kid grow up before you. You're thinking you're still a young guy and then realize the five-year-old you used to teach is now driving. The other teachers and I came here in our twenties, and now we're all either turning gray or we've lost our hair. With the kids, we're like a family growing older together.

I think about how Brittany might have grown up under different circumstances, but I try not to play the What if? game. I remember her up to age three and have very fond memories of those years. I remember her standing up for the first time. I remember getting her ears pierced. I remember how she rolled with me to comedy clubs, the waitstaff watching her while I performed. I remember her coming out to meet us when we picked her up from the babysitter, as if she heard us coming up the steps and knew: *That's my parents.* All of these are warm memories. What fills my heart outweighs the sadness.

For years I dreamed about Brittany. I still do. I imagine her living, growing up, and talking like she never could. She wouldn't be saying just anything. She'd be repeating phrases and thoughts that she might have heard from Brigitte and me. I always wonder about that: What would she say that we'd know came from us?

Since we liked to dance around the house, would she be doing that too?

Brittany was my mom's oldest grandchild, so as I watch my brother's children grow up, I think of where she would have been in life in relation to her cousins. She was older than they were, so they would have looked up to her.

She would be tall because Brigitte is tall and I'm tall. She would have long hair, and she would be intelligent, and that's because of Brigitte.

And she would be chill, and that's because of me.

Sometimes I see girls in grade school, and afterward I tell Brigitte, "Man, there was a girl who looked just like Brittany: her skin tone, complexion, long hair . . ."

It doesn't make me sad. To try to renegotiate life or think about what might have been could drive me crazy.

The fact is, I am who I am, and I'm doing what I'm doing. This is my life. I'm older and wiser. What has been is what forms me. Mentally, spiritually, and physically, it makes me who I am.

I've met couples who have broken up after a tragedy hits. They try to act as if it never happened. A child might pass, or a parent might pass, and they don't have pictures of that person anymore. With Brigitte and me, Brittany was a part of our life. She shaped us. She's still with us.

When I asked God why Brigitte and I are still together, He revealed to me, *I saw that you two were strong and should be able to handle this.*

This got me to thinking. Brigitte grew up in an abusive household, which made her strong, and I grew up around strong women, which made me strong—not physical strength so much as inner strength. Now you have two people together who grew up individually strong, so when something happens to test us, it just makes us stronger.

God sees the past, present, and future all at once. He knew that in the future Brigitte and I would find out what He already knew about us. What we went through was horrific, and we'd never choose to endure it under any circumstances. But Brigitte and I relied on each other, and that strengthened both of us. When we reach the end of our life's journey, we'll realize: *Man, I'm stronger.* God always knew it.

If I could, I'd go back to tell young Brigitte and Anthony how she'll eventually feel like a surrogate mom in her job, and I'll feel like a surrogate father as a Sunday school teacher. I'd also say that during those times when we can't find our footing, we should know that God is carrying us.

Brigitte

Anthony and I have been married for thirty-one years, and we've known each other for thirty-four years, and I have never doubted that we'd stay together. The most important thing we share is core values. Of course, he makes me laugh. Of course, he's nice to me and other people, but to me that's kind of superficial— because if you don't have those other core values, then when a conflict occurs, the relationship is over no matter how funny or nice someone is.

Religion is a significant one for us. He is very involved in the church while I pray and study the Scriptures more on my own, but we share faith at our core. If we did not, that would have been a deal breaker.

Trust is another core connector. I don't think I would have been able to stay in a marriage if there were a high degree of jealousy. I don't respond well to that.

It's also important to be able to fight fairly and to relate to the other person's point of view without necessarily having to agree with it. As connected as the two of us are, we each need some autonomy. Anthony has his set of friends who are single and married, and I have my set of friends who are single and married, and then we have mutual friendships.

One other pillar is what you bring to the relationship from your childhood and how that translates into being a parent. I had a traumatizing childhood and have tried to compensate ever since. Anthony adored his mom, who was such an incredible woman, and he brought her great qualities to our family.

Anthony

We balance each other out. Some men fear Brigitte, and I always say, "Really?" When she's not with me, she's formidable, a force of nature, which is how I saw her in the beginning. But to me, she's quiet, warm, and gentle.

We're good together. I'll give her thirty more years.

Brigitte

Anthony's illness definitely affects our relationship. I've got to be his caregiver as well as his partner, and that complicates matters and adds stress. I worry not only about something happening to him but also about something happening to me. What would he do if I weren't here? I like to be ready for any shoe that might drop.

It makes my heart a little sad to see how his fine-motor skills and gross-motor skills have become diminished, but he still has the same spirit and the same drive for independence. He has slowed down, and his delivery of humor is different, but I like the way he has adjusted to accommodate for his challenges. It's now part of him, and it's awesome.

Anthony

The disease's progression does not scare me because I'm surrounded by people who love me. I think that doctors will find a cure, and, in the meantime, technology is here to help.

Brigitte

Anthony can't wait to get one of those autonomous vehicles. My response: "I don't think so."

Anyway, if I had to use a word or two to sum up how I'm feeling about our future, I'd say, "cautiously hopeful." We're putting things in place and getting prepared.

Anthony

I would say "hopeful" without "cautiously." I'm more positive.

The through line remains faith.

Brigitte

Faith and preparation.

Anthony

Preparation faith.

Brigitte

That sounds like a cream or an ointment.

Anthony

Though you have faith, you still prepare. You don't have blind faith without doing anything. You can't think God's going to get you a house while you're not saving money for it.

Brigitte

When you look at everything we have faced in our marriage, it either makes it or breaks it. It's like going to war with a platoon buddy. If we can get through this, we can kick ass. We got this. Yup?

Anthony

Yup.

Brigitte

We got this. You don't go that far just to throw in the chips. Some people break up because their partner snores or farts a lot. Those kinds of issues are silly to me because we've been through some serious stuff, right? I know it's their journey, but our journey was one that we could compare it to and say to the other couple: "You know what? Snap out of it. Get it together. Go in the back room and hug it out because it could be worse. It could be worse."

Anthony

I've been married now for thirty-one years, and if my wife gets mad at me, she does retail therapy. Whatever she brings back home, I can't say anything. She got a Great Dane with a small pooper scooper with my name on it. And every day that dog comes to me with that pooper scooper.

I finish up my Comedy & Magic Club set, watch my fellow comics' sets, and say my goodbyes. Mike lets me order an extra pasta dish to bring home to Brigitte, who still doesn't like coming out to the clubs when she doesn't have to. I can't wait to get home to tell her about the night.

I don't feel sorry for us. I feel lucky.

I have a beautiful woman who's been with me for more than thirty years, who's been at my side through all of this. When I turn around, she's still here. She still laughs at my stupid jokes. I'm not the wealthiest guy around, but she has committed to the ride, and that's a great blessing.

Happiness is a quality you have, not something that's conditional.

I was a happy kid.

I'm still happy.

About the Authors

Anthony Griffith, a successful stand-up comedian for more than thirty years, made his way from Chicago's South Side to the city's comedy clubs and out to Los Angeles, where he performed multiple times on *The Tonight Show* with Johnny Carson and later with Jay Leno. He has been featured in specials for Comedy Central, HBO, and Showtime and on *The Arsenio Hall Show*. Also an actor, Griffith has appeared in several movies, including *Panther, Tales from the Hood*, and *Charlie's Angels: Full Throttle*, and received a Daytime Emmy for his performance in the TV movie *Our Father*. Griffith also performed in the TV series *Curb Your Enthusiasm* and *The Bernie Mac Show*.

Dr. Brigitte Travis-Griffin is a clinical psychologist specializing in a concierge delivery system of therapy for entertainment and creative professionals. She and Anthony Griffith have been married for more than thirty years. Brigitte received her PsyD from the California School of Professional Psychology and her BS from UCLA.

Mark Caro is the award-winning author of *The Foie Gras Wars* and *Take It to the Bridge: Unlocking the Great Songs Inside You*. For more than twenty-five years, he covered entertainment, food, and culture for the *Chicago Tribune*. He continues to contribute to the *New York Times*, *Chicago* magazine, and other publications.